MILLION DOLLAR BRAND

Build a Profitable Brand You Own,
Create Your Dream Lifestyle, and
Achieve Financial Freedom Forever

Matt Clark

AMAZING

Disclaimer: Before we jump into showing you how to build your own business, you need to understand something: there are no guarantees in business. Your results will be highly dependent on your effort, persistence, and even some amount of luck. Some people who follow what you'll learn in this book will make little to no money. However, we believe the potential reward is worth the risk.

INTRODUCTION: "HOW DO YOU REALLY **MAKE MONEY** IN BUSINESS?"

In my first job out of college, I worked at an investment bank. It was the "safe" job, and on paper everything seemed great. But inside, it was killing me.

The 16-hour days were unfulfilling and soul-sucking. What's more, working for someone else and lining *their* pockets didn't feel right. I felt like I was working my butt off as a cog in the wheel. I wanted to control my own future, decide how and when I would work, and reap the rewards of my contribution. I wanted to make my own way.

So I quit. I fumbled my way into ecommerce and became obsessed with figuring out how to build a successful business. Because I really didn't know what I was doing, I tried and failed a lot. I started over twenty businesses in four years.

In one of my early businesses, I achieved two million dollars in revenue in the second year of operations. Sounds great right? Except for one thing... there was no profit.

I was so anxious to generate sales, I figured I'd worry about profit in my self-funded venture later on. The result: massive credit card debt.

My back was against the wall. So I dug in harder. I went to conferences, joined masterminds, took online courses, and read every business and self-development book I could get my hands on. Yet no one could answer my question: *how do you really make money in business?*

It became clear that no one was going to swoop in and give me the answer. I had to figure it out for myself. So I began testing, trying, and failing. I made mistakes, but I learned as I went, and in time, I found the answers for myself. It became clear to me exactly how to make an online business work. I figured out how to not only get lots of sales, but also how to make *real profit*, all while enjoying the personal freedom and flexibility I came to love from having my own successful business.

Once I figured things out, I wasn't content to keep what I learned to myself. Why should other people have to learn the hard way, like I did? Why not save them the same blood, sweat, and tears that I'd spent?

I wanted to do more than just make money, I wanted to show others what I'd discovered to help them improve their lives. Around that time, I met Jason, now my business partner, in a mastermind group. Like me, Jason had previously worked for a large corporation and come to the conclusion that it just wasn't for him. He'd been working his way up the corporate ladder to provide for his young family. At one point, the company cut all bonuses while the CEO got a multi-million dollar payout. That's when Jason decided he didn't want to work so hard just to make someone else rich. At nights and on the weekends, he studied and tested methods to build an online business. After a few years, he made it work. He quit his job and made more money working for himself than he'd ever made working at his corporate job.

Jason and I decided to join together to combine our knowledge into a course. From the very beginning, we took the stance that the course must not be focused on teaching—it must be focused on *doing*. I knew from personal experience that someone trying to build a business doesn't want a degree or a certificate for their knowledge—they want to *actually build a business*! With that in mind, we structured the course so that it was laid out in bite-sized chunks, followed by real-world business implementation. The goal was that by the end of the eight-week online training, the person going through the course would have built a real, highly successful business. This was the foundation of our training program we later called Amazing Selling Machine (ASM).

The results of this approach and the course we created together absolutely astounded us. People that had spent years "trying everything"—including one guy who told me he'd tried to build similar businesses for 12 long years and had never seen results—were using our method to make insane profits and build life-changing businesses for themselves.

One of our first big successes was a pastor at the time. He was living with his wife and kids in government-subsidized housing, getting by on a meager income. He took our training, and within six months had built a business generating over $100,000 per month in sales, and more than $35,000 a month in profit. He even paid cash for a new house for his family. Today he still owns his business—and based on what I know about his sales, it's worth around $13 million.

> ## Once I figured things out, I wasn't content to keep what I learned to myself.

Since joining together, Jason and I have reached millions of people with our videos teaching how to build successful businesses. We've personally helped over 30,000 people discover how to build their own brands. We estimate that the people we've taught have sold over $8.69 billion through their own businesses. They've come from all different backgrounds and levels of experience, from teachers to doctors to veterans, as well as countless others.

For example, one current student, Ana Silva, is an Assistant Director at a university. She had never built an ecommerce business before, but with her new business she's sold as much as $100,000 in a single month online.

And then there's Galya and her husband Andrei. Their goal was to make enough money so Andrei could leave his truck driving job and be at home with their family more often. Their business has done as much as $130,000 in a single month and is on-track to sell over a million dollars this year.

Because of this successes like these, Amazing.com has been featured in nearly every major business publication including: Forbes, CNBC, Business Insider, Success Magazine, Entrepreneur, Time, and Startup Nation. We've been published alongside other experts such as Gary Vaynerchuk, Grant Cardone, Bethenny Frankel, and Dave Asprey. We've worked closely with others who share our mission to help people improve their lives through entrepreneurship such as: Sir Richard Branson, Founder of the Virgin Group, Robert Kiyosaki, author of *Rich Dad Poor Dad*, Sara Blakely, Founder of Spanx, Inc., Dave Asprey, Founder of Bulletproof, and John Mackey, Founder of Whole Foods, the healthy grocery chain that sold to Amazon for $13.4 billion.

Today, Jason and I estimate that the people who have been through our training generate over one billion dollars in sales every year. We've helped people from over one hundred and thirty-eight countries build businesses. And we estimate we've helped create over one thousand millionaires.

But why stop there? I know there are many more people out there—people like you—who could also benefit from this knowledge. So I took some of the most essential and powerful strategies from our training programs and turned them into this book. With this book, you can get started immediately, without waiting one second longer to create your dream life.

HOW JENNA AND TRAVIS ZIGLER TURNED THEIR PASSION & EXPERTISE INTO MILLIONS OF DOLLARS… AND A MEANINGFUL CHARITY.

By most people's assessments, Dr. Jenna Zigler and Travis Zigler were already successful.

As optometrists in Columbus, Ohio, they ran two highly profitable practices, and they liked their jobs well enough. But there was a catch.

"It was time intensive," says Travis. "You had to go in to see patients to make money. One day, we did an analysis of stress versus money made." They didn't like what they saw: too much stress, for not enough money.

They decided to sell their practices and start a new business that would give them the financial freedom and lifestyle they really wanted for themselves. They chose to focus full-time on an online business, using our training as their guide.

"We followed the course exactly on how to pick a product. Along the way we thought, 'why not pick something that is in our area of expertise?'. And that's what we did. So our first product was polarized sunglasses."

Since starting with that single product, Jenna and Travis have sold their optometry practices and grew their brand to include up to 70 different products at a time. Their product line is focused on something they know and care a lot about: eye care.

"Our goal with our business today is to help people heal their dry eyes naturally. We've helped over 50,000 people, and we're trying to help one million."

While pursuing a goal they're passionate about, their business has continued to grow. "We did $86,000 in sales in 2015; $1.2 million in 2016; $2.5 million in 2017; and $3.6 million in 2018." For 2019, the Zigler's anticipate $4 million from Amazon sales alone.

Meanwhile, they're also finding success by selling on their own website. "Our website is currently doing about $2,500-$3,000 per day and it will probably overtake [our] Amazon [sales] by the end of the year."

Jenna and Travis are not only making more money, these days they're working a lot less. They typically work six to seven hours a day, for about three days a week.

But they're quick to acknowledge they did work hard to get here. "You have to have dedication and perseverance. I think that's one of the things that made us so successful right from the beginning," says Jenna. "We woke up every single day and we watched the training videos. We got home from work after seeing patients all day and we watched more videos. And we implemented every single thing that ASM taught us to do—and that's exactly how our business became what it is today."

Perhaps best of all, the Ziglers are using their profits to fund their own charity, the Eye Love Cares Foundation. "We use the funds from the donation to help fund clinics in developing countries for people that can no longer afford or obtain eye care. We focus on the island of Jamaica and hope to build sustainable clinics there in our lifetime."

"[Having a charity like this] is something we hoped we get to at the age of 60—and here we are in our mid-thirties already hitting this goal."

Whether you've never built a business before, you've tried building a business and failed, or you own a business but feel like you're stuck and not getting the freedom you want, this book is for you. The methods you'll learn will enable you to run a profitable business by creating your own brand and selling online using Amazon, the world's largest online retailer. All of which can be done from your own home, or anywhere around the world.

With what you learn in this book you will:

- Choose the right products to sell
- Find high-quality suppliers for any product
- Get people to buy your products (and even beat big brands on Amazon)
- Maximize profitability and scale your business to meet your dreams and goals
- Put a 12-month roadmap in place so you know exactly what to do and when

I'll walk you through every step, and give you some tools to help you put what you learn into action. Along the way, you'll also hear stories about people who have done this before, so you can learn (and gain inspiration!) from their experience.

When you put what you learn in this book into action, you'll finally have the freedom to do *what* you want, *when* you want. And that freedom is really why you're here, isn't it? By reading this book and taking action on what you learn, you're voting in favor of your own freedom— the kind of freedom you've only dreamt of. You can replace or exceed income from your existing job, achieve financial security, and be your own boss. With this freedom you can spend more time with your family, travel the world, live wherever you want, and do whatever you want.

Even better? Building a business and creating freedom for yourself doesn't just improve your life, it improves the lives of your family members, your friends, your community, the employees you hire, your customers, and those touched by the ripple effect of your success.

It all begins with the simple business model of making small improvements to existing products. That's it. That's how you build a million dollar brand from scratch.

The best part? You can get started right now.

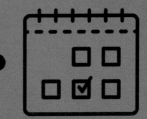

THE BEST BUSINESS
TO START **TODAY.**

Picture this... you're on vacation with those you love. Before heading out to explore the sites and go on new adventures, you check the stats of your new business.

You see you've made sales overnight. While you were sleeping, customers across the world paid you money.

You didn't have to do anything to make those sales. You set up the system months before and now your income grows around the clock whether you're at home, with your family, or traveling the world.

You're no longer tied down to a set location or schedule—and you definitely don't have to answer to a "boss" anymore.

You've escaped the daily grind, the endless cycle of waking up, working for someone else, squeezing out a tiring hour or two at night to take care of chores, and repeating the whole thing over again the next day.

You're doing what you want to do with your life. You don't have to worry about bills. You don't have to miss out on important life experiences being trapped in an office.

You're free to live your life, have fun, enjoy the things you love, and, best of all, provide for those you love most.

How did you do it?

You learned how to build a cash-producing brand that *you own*. With that knowledge, you created a business that works for you around the clock—and can be run from anywhere in the world. With just a laptop and an internet connection, you created your own freedom.

This new life starts today.

Your current reality may be far from what's possible with this business. You might even feel trapped and hopeless. And you might be unsure how you'll ever get out of the daily grind.

But that can change faster than you might imagine.

To create the life you want, the solution is simple.

To change your life and get out of the daily grind, you need three things:

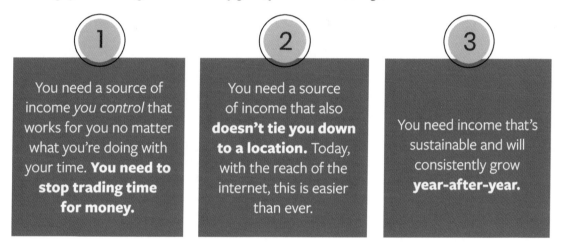

1 You need a source of income *you control* that works for you no matter what you're doing with your time. **You need to stop trading time for money.**

2 You need a source of income that also **doesn't tie you down to a location.** Today, with the reach of the internet, this is easier than ever.

3 You need income that's sustainable and will consistently grow **year-after-year.**

In this book, I'll show you how to accomplish each of these steps and how to build a business selling products with a brand that YOU own, leveraging the power of the world's largest online retailer.

But first, let's consider the opportunity in front of you.

For the average person who wants to make money by building a profitable business, this is the best time in history.

Consider this: chances are you do some (maybe most) of your shopping online. Almost every large retailer, and even many small, family-owned stores, have an online shop. So it may surprise you that online retail is still in its infancy. For the US, in 2008, online retail represented only 5.3% of total retail. By 2018, online retail's share of total retail nearly tripled to 14.3%. Brick-and-mortar retail sales are shifting quickly online, but online retail sales are still a small fraction of total retail sales. Big companies who have built their businesses based on the old model over the last fifty to a hundred years are terrified — the new world of online retail isn't built for them.

In the past, all the power went to big brands with big budgets who could get their products into the limited space available at big retailers like Walmart. Today, with the infinite reach of the internet and infinite digital "shelf space" available, that's all changed. The power is now in the hands of the person with the right product for the right audience with the right marketing strategies.

For a big brand, these opportunities are small. If you're a $300 billion giant like Procter & Gamble, you don't have the time for a "measly" $2 million opportunity. But, for a single entrepreneur with zero, or just a handful of employees, that's a life-changing amount of money that can set you free for life.

Your money-making business model: a snap-shot.

The business model that we've used to sell millions online across multiple brands (and have taught others how to use too) involves selling real, tangible products under a real brand that you own.

Some of the biggest brands in the world like Apple, Nike, 3M, Nestlé, L'OREAL, and Johnson & Johnson have been built following the same model of selling consumer products. Look around you right now—whether you're in your home, office, or out in public, there are hundreds or even thousands of physical goods that fill the space you're in and make your life better, easier, or more fun.

HOW JUSTIN AND CHANNING DYSON SET A NEW COURSE FOR THEIR LIVES.

Just a few short years ago, Justin and Channing were living a very different life.

Justin was going back to college for mobile development while also working for his dad. His wife, Channing, was working 50 hours a week as a hairstylist. They were both 23 years old, living in a starter home in Nevada, Texas with their four-year-old. They knew they wanted a different sort of life—a life that would allow them to travel, spend quality time with their family, and make *real* money without slogging away at a regular job. But they couldn't figure out how to make it happen.

When they heard about our training through best-selling personal finance author Robert Kiyosaki, they decided to give it a try.

Flashforward to today. The Dysons now own a brand selling over half-a-million dollars a month. Their gross profit each month: over $225,000.

"I've made more money in a single month than I used to make in a year," says Channing. "We travel almost every month, sometimes more than once. We can take the day off and go do fun stuff with our kids whenever we want."

How'd they do it?

While they now they have 79 SKUs (products), Channing and Justin started their brand with just one product: a car seat cover. At first, they admit choosing a product felt a bit intimidating. "There are lots of options, so analysis paralysis can definitely set in. But like anything else, if you just commit to moving forward then you'll figure things out along the way. And we did."

Once they launched their product, it didn't take long for sales to take off. "We listed our product on Amazon and turned on Amazon ads. A sale or two came in the first couple days and things ramped up from there."

To focus on the business, Justin quit his job and dropped out of college. During the first six months after launching the business, they'd spend about 40-50 hours a week working on it. Now their work week is a more manageable 30-40 hours and highly flexible.

The profits speak for themselves. "Last year we sold about $4 million and this year we should sell more than $6 million of our products. Gross profit is usually around 40%."

But Justin and Channing consider this just the beginning. "We enjoy running the company, so the plan is to keep growing it and learn as much as we can. We'll eventually sell it and probably just start over with more capital and experience to work with than we did the first time."

Their words of advice? "Most people agree that time is worth more than money, but they willingly trade their time for money for over half their lifetime. This business allows you to put your money to work so you can keep your time. I don't know of a more powerful reason than that to make the decision to invest in yourself and build something that will work for you, not the other way around. Your family deserves that. You deserve that. Trust yourself and you will make it a reality."

With this business, you'll sell high-quality products under your own brand. You'll tap into an existing customer base of 200 million people looking to buy products like yours.

Best of all, you own the brand yourself. This is not a multi-level marketing business where you sell someone else's products to your friends and family members. This is a real business, selling real products to customers already looking to buy.

Because you own the brand, you have two ways to make money with this business: First, when your business succeeds, you profit from the monthly sales your business makes, putting money into your pocket each and every month. Second, because you own a cash-producing asset, you can sell this business in the future for up to five times the amount of money it makes every year.

To make this business model work you need to do a few things correctly:

- You need to choose the right products to sell.

- You need to source those products from high-quality suppliers and manufacturers.

- You need to effectively brand and market those products first on Amazon.
  (Why Amazon in particular, you ask? I'll answer that in Chapter 2.)

- Finally, you need to scale your business according to your goals, so you can achieve the financial freedom, and life, you want for yourself.

In the coming chapters I'll show you how to do all of these things, step-by-step. But to make this work, I need you to do one thing first.

FAQ: WHY BOTHER RUNNING A BUSINESS WHEN YOU COULD JUST BE AN EMPLOYEE?

Simply put, there are three main advantages to building a business versus working as an employee when it comes to building wealth.

These are:

1. The unlimited upside potential to make as much income as *you* want.

2. Wealth building: you own the asset (the business) which can be sold in the future.

3. Time freedom: You have the ability to hire people to run the business for you so it makes money without you having to settle for trading your time for money.

Before you read on, I need your commitment.

Real learning doesn't take place unless it changes your behavior. I don't care what you *know* after you read this book, I care *what you do* after you read it.

In other words... Thinking alone isn't going to do anything for you. Wishing and wanting for something to be different won't help.

What *will* help?

Doing the work. I'm giving you the best strategies I have for quickly building a successful business online. I'm not holding the most profitable strategies back.

I'm giving you all this because, months from now, I want to see you financially free and living an amazing life.

So, before we go any further, I'm going to ask for your commitment. I want you to tell me right here, right now, that you will take what I teach you in this book and use it to improve the quality of your life. Do we have a deal?

Take the "Next Action" below, and then keep on reading.

YOUR NEXT ACTION: MAKE A COMMITMENT.

Make a decision right now to commit to taking action on the strategies in this book.

If you're committed, write down the following in your notebook and sign it — or sign right here in the book.

> *"I commit to taking action to build a business with what I learn in the Million Dollar Brand book so I can improve the quality of my own life."*
>
> *— Signed,* _____
> *(your name)*
>
> *on* _____
> *(today's date)*

THE PERFECT
PRODUCT OPPORTUNITY:

THE 5 CRITERIA TO FIND
PRODUCTS YOU *KNOW*
WILL *SELL*.

02

So you're going to build a business selling products online. Where do you start?

First, you need to find a good product opportunity. Today, this is incredibly simple and fast to do because so many online sales happen in one place, on one website.

In the U.S., 50% of all sales online happen on one website: Amazon.com. But Amazon isn't just a U.S. ecommerce marketplace. People buy billions of dollars of products on Amazon in the U.K., Germany, all over the rest of Europe, Japan, India, and more.

Even if you don't live in the U.S., or in any of the areas of the world where Amazon is the dominant marketplace, you can still take advantage of this massive marketplace. We've helped people from 138 countries do just that.

FAQ: WHY SELL ON AMAZON?

As you've just learned, 50% of all online sales in the U.S. take place on Amazon.com. And internationally, people buy extensively on Amazon too. That makes it the go-to platform for selling just about any product.

Amazon is the best place to start selling products online because they take care of a lot of the hassle of running an online business for you. You won't have to take care of website maintenance, website security, credit card processor setup and maintenance, chargebacks, or dealing with fraudulent orders.

Plus, when you use Amazon to warehouse your inventory and ship out your orders, like you'll learn soon, they take care of the majority of your customer service. Most customer service concerns are related to shipping, which Amazon handles themselves!

As you'll read, many successful business owners ultimately choose to branch out and sell their products on other platforms too—and I encourage you to do the same. But for the fastest and easiest success, start with Amazon.

How to create an Amazon Seller Central account.

To sell on Amazon, you need a Seller Central account. This type of account is different than the one you use to buy products on Amazon as a customer.

You don't need to set this account up until after you've decided on a product to sell. However, I want to give this information to you now so you're clear on *how* the process of selling on Amazon works before you start looking for *what* you're going to sell.

There are four main Amazon marketplaces that produce the majority of sales: Amazon.com (US), Amazon.co.uk (UK), Amazon.de (Germany), and Amazon.co.jp (Japan).

Unless you live in the UK, Germany, or Japan, we recommend you sell on Amazon.com in the US because it's the marketplace that produces the majority (60%) of Amazon's sales.

This means if you live anywhere in the US or anywhere *other than* the UK, Germany, or Japan, you'll head on over to https://sellercentral.amazon.com to create an account to sell on Amazon. If you live in one of the other three areas, then you can start by selling on your local Amazon marketplace by visiting its Seller Central website: https://sellercentral.amazon.co.uk/, https://sellercentral.amazon.co.jp/, or https://sellercentral.amazon.de/.

We recommend that you create a *Professional account* from the beginning. The cost is low — only about $40 per month — and this account type includes features you'll need to follow the model you learn about in this book.

In most cases, you can create your Seller Central account under your personal name without creating a legal business entity. Later, when you're ready, you can create a company such as a Limited Liability Company (LLC) and add that information to your Seller Central account so payments are then received by and charged to your company for greater tax efficiency and legal protection.

Remember, you can create your Seller Central account after you've found a product opportunity. There's nothing you need to do inside Seller Central until your inventory is ordered. However, now you know the process and can come back to it at anytime.

Now that you know what type of account you need to sell on Amazon, what exactly do you sell?

So you *can* sell on Amazon. But what exactly do you sell?

The five critical criteria you must use when choosing a product.

Any product you choose should meet five specific criteria to ensure you will be successful from the start. This is critical–don't skip a single one of these criteria. These were developed through years of experience selling on Amazon, as well as helping thousands of other people find their profitable products.

The five criteria are:

1. Your product should have a Best Sellers Rank (BSR) between 300-5,000. (Don't worry, I'll explain BSR in a moment.)

2. The product's selling price range should be between $15 to $70. Going any lower than this can mean your product will not have a big enough profit, and going higher can make your first inventory costs too high.

3. The product should have 1,000 reviews or less. This is an indicator the competition level is low enough that you will be able to launch and compete relatively easily.

4. The product should be less than five pounds in weight.

5. You must be able to private label the product and sell it under your own brand. This is absolutely critical for anyone looking to make serious money selling their own physical products. Instead of competing with hundreds of other sellers all selling the exact same product, you are able to create your own version of a product with your own brand name, packaging, and label on it. Eventually, you'll make improvements to your product to give your customers more value than your competitors.

You now know the five critical criteria that you use when searching for products. In a moment, I'll show you exactly how to find a product that meets all these criteria. But first, let's have a closer look at Best Sellers Rank, or BSR.

Best Sellers Rank (BSR)

If you know what to look for, you can find thousands of product opportunities on Amazon— and it's all publicly available information.

Amazon ranks all the products on its marketplaces by the number of units sold. It calls this the Best Sellers Rank, or BSR. By looking at the BSR, you can figure out which products sell the best, in any category, on Amazon in minutes.

Here's how it works. Amazon shows a product's BSR on the product listing page. This is depicted by a number, with 1 being the best-selling. I recommend you choose a product that has a BSR between 300 and 5,000. The reason for this range is that you want to find a product that has high demand, but low competition. A product that is ranked beyond 5,000 may not have enough demand, or sales volume. A product that is ranked lower than 300 may be too competitive.

To see BSR, simply click on a product on Amazon. Then, about halfway down the page, near the product description, you'll see a section called *Product details* or *Product information*. That's where you'll find BSR.

Product details
   Product Dimensions: 2.7 x 1.2 x 5.4 inches ; 4.6 ounces
   Shipping Weight: 3.2 ounces (View shipping rates and policies)
   ASIN: B07R5KYCL3
   UPC: 855502008524
   Average Customer Review: ★★★★☆ ˅   544 customer reviews
   Amazon Best Sellers Rank: #773 in Beauty & Personal Care (See Top 100 in Beauty & Personal Care)
      #14 in Deodorants
   Would you like to **tell us about a lower price**?

As you can see in the example above, at the time this screenshot was taken, this product was number 773 in Beauty & Personal Care. Beauty & Personal Care products is a top level category. You can always tell which category is top level, as it will be listed first and have "See Top 100" in whatever category it is.

Underneath that, it shows #14 in Deodorants. This is a sub-category, which you can ignore.

As I mentioned earlier, having a good BSR is the first criteria that your product must meet. In the example below, you can see that this product satisfies that requirement—it has a great BSR. It is the 1,033rd best selling product in the Office Products category.

ASIN	B01GDJ2BH6
Customer Reviews	★★★★☆ ˅ 402 customer reviews 4.4 out of 5 stars
Best Sellers Rank	#1,033 in Office Products (See Top 100 in Office Products) #1 in Bar Code Scanners
Shipping Weight	11.2 ounces (View shipping rates and policies)
Date First Available	May 31, 2016

Using this method, you won't have to wonder whether a product will sell well—you'll know for a fact that people are buying it using this data.

The one piece of information Amazon doesn't give you is the estimated amount of sales for each corresponding BSR. Amazon keeps this data private. However, a couple years ago we invested in a software company that has proprietary data and can accurately estimate the sales for any product on Amazon. One of their tools is completely free and gives you this data. You'll learn more about it soon, but, when you're ready, you can access it here: www.MillionDollarBrandBook.com/finder

Just remember, your goal is to find product opportunities with high sales and low competition. After that, you create your own brand of a similar, ideally better value product, and start profiting from the opportunity.

Let's walk through the specific steps to find great product opportunities using Amazon that meet all five of the criteria requirements.

How to find a product that meets your five critical criteria

To find a product that meets all of your criteria, head over to Amazon. Once there, you'll want to do a product search using something called a search string. The search string is the minus (-) symbol, followed by seven or more random characters that do not make up a real word. This string enables you to see nearly all the products in a category, without restricting them with a normal keyword. (You can see an example in the image below.)

Once you've entered your search string, select a category on the left.

The categories we recommend you focus on include the following:

- Arts, Crafts, & Sewing
- Home & Kitchen
- Automotive*
- Industrial & Scientific
- Baby
- Kitchen & Housewares
- Beauty
- Musical Instruments
- Camera & Photo
- Office Products

- Cell Phones & Accessories
- Patio, Lawn, & Garden
- Computers
- Pet Supplies
- Electronics
- Sports & Outdoors
- Grocery & Gourmet Food*
- Tools & Hardware
- Health & Household
- Toys & Games

Categories with an asterisk require approval from Amazon. Please note that some sub-categories in Beauty and Health & Household do require approval, although the main categories themselves do not.

Then, once you've chosen your category, hit the search button — i.e. the magnifying glass. In the example above, I've selected 'Home and Kitchen'.

This initial search delivers a *lot* of products to choose from. As you can see below, my example search generated 50,000 results. Going through every single one of those results to evaluate how it measures up against your criteria would be overwhelming and incredibly time consuming.

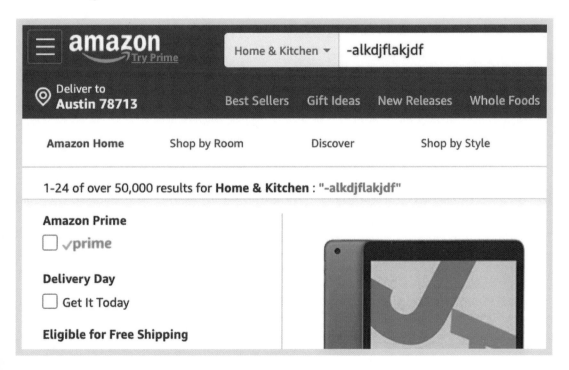

Fortunately, we have a special tool to help you simplify this process: a special product research extension for Google Chrome.

LET'S GET SEARCHING! GET YOUR PRODUCT RESEARCH EXTENSION NOW.

To get the special Google Chrome browser extension I just described go here: **www.MillionDollarBrandBook.com/finder**

Let's take a look at how the extension works. You can see the extension in the top right of the image below.

When you click on the extension, it goes through the entire page and pulls all the search results. (As you can see below.)

Once you've searched using the product research extension, the next thing to do is click on the bottom left button that says "load next page." Then you just have to wait for it to pull all the products from the next page, which it does very quickly. In the example below, I've loaded 5 pages, and as you can see, there are 120 products in the extension. This would typically take you a long time, but with the product research extension you can do this in about a minute.

#	Product Name	Brand	Price	Category	Rank	Mo. Sales	Revenue	Reviews	Rating	Weight
AD	[2 Pack] Benazcap Screen Prot...	Benazcap	$13.99	N/A	N/A	N/A	N/A	1	5.0	0.49 lbs
1	New Apple iPad (10.2-Inch, Wi...	Apple	$328.41	N/A	N/A	N/A	N/A	24	4.4	N/A
2	Apple AirPods with Charging C...	Apple	$144.00	N/A	N/A	N/A	N/A	3,159	4.4	N/A
3	Apple Watch Series 5 (GPS, 44...	Apple	$414.00	N/A	N/A	N/A	N/A	61	4.3	N/A
4	Apple Watch Series 3 (GPS, 38...	Apple	$189.00	N/A	N/A	N/A	N/A	3,683	4.6	N/A
5	Apple AirPods with Wireless C...	Apple	$169.00	N/A	N/A	N/A	N/A	1,045	4.4	N/A
6	Apple Watch Series 5 (GPS + C...	Apple	$514.00	N/A	N/A	N/A	N/A	22	4.4	N/A
7	Powerbeats Pro - Totally Wirel...	Beats	$199.95	N/A	N/A	N/A	N/A	785	5.0	N/A
8	Apple TV 4K (64GB, Latest Mo...	Apple	$199.00	N/A	N/A	N/A	N/A	1,280	4.4	N/A
9	Samsung SSD 860 EVO 1TB 2...	Samsung	$129.99	N/A	N/A	N/A	N/A	6,522	4.7	0.11 lbs
10	hOmeLabs 3,000 Sq. Ft Energ...	hOmeLabs	$189.99	Home & Kit...	#112	12,317	$2,340,107	4,473	4.5	40 lbs
11	Samsung T5 Portable SSD - 2T...	Samsung	$279.99	N/A	N/A	N/A	N/A	2,196	4.6	0.1 lbs

Profit Miner (showing results for "-alkdjflakjdf") Ads Images Filters Averages Get Free Training Help ×

Load next page » Loaded 5 pages (showing 120 products and 45 Ad products)

Once that's done, you can now filter all the results based on the criteria I shared with you earlier. To do that, click on "Filters", located in the top right. Then, put the criteria into the filter boxes it opens up. I'll walk you through this step-by-step.

The first filter we want to put into place is price. As per the example below, I've set the price for $15-$70, the range mentioned in the critical criteria listed above. Remember, this range makes sure you have a high enough potential profit to make you significant income and keeps your inventory costs manageable.

	Product Name	Brand	Price ∨	Category	Rank	Mo. Sales	Revenue	Reviews	Rating	Weight
Min	Include	Include	15	Include	Min	Min	Min	Min	Min	Min
Max	Exclude	Exclude	70	Exclude	Max	Max	Max	Max	Max	Max
AD	ZtotopCase for New iPad 7th ...	ZtotopCase	$16.99	N/A	N/A	N/A	N/A	34	4.6	1.55 lbs
AD	DTTO New iPad 7th Generatio...	DTTO	$17.99	N/A	N/A	N/A	N/A	12	4.7	0.99 lbs
AD	TiMOVO Case for New iPad 7t...	TiMOVO	$15.79	N/A	N/A	N/A	N/A	3	2.5	0.41 lbs
AD	BERSEM Screen Protector for i...	BERSEM	$19.99	N/A	N/A	N/A	N/A	1	3.0	0.22 lbs
AD	Ztotop for iPad 10.2 Case 201...	ZtotopCase	$21.99	N/A	N/A	N/A	N/A	6	5.0	0.75 lbs
AD	YUNTAB Android 4.4 Q88 Tabl...	YUNTAB	$45.99	Computers ...	#28,062	11	$506	7	4.6	1.3 lbs
AD	ZtotopCase for New iPad 7th ...	ZtotopCase	$21.99	N/A	N/A	N/A	N/A	34	4.6	0.7 lbs
AD	YUNTAB 7-inch Q88H Kids Tab...	YUNTAB	$53.99	N/A	N/A	N/A	N/A	0	0.0	1.66 lbs
41	Fire TV Stick with Alexa Voice ...	Amazon	$39.99	N/A	N/A	N/A	N/A	39,373	4.5	N/A
AD	Ztotop Case for iPad 10.2 Inch ...	ZtotopCase	$15.99	N/A	N/A	N/A	N/A	25	4.5	0.64 lbs
AD	GUDOU 2019 New iPad 7th Ge...	GUDOU	$15.99	N/A	N/A	N/A	N/A	0	4.9	0.74 lbs

Profit Miner (showing results for "-alkdjflakjdf") Ads Images Filters Averages Get Free Training Help ×

Next, enter a BSR between 300 to 5,000.

#	Product Name	Brand	Price	Category	Rank	Mo. Sales	Revenue	Reviews	Rating	Weight
Min	Include	Include	15	Include	300	Min	Min	Min	Min	Min
Max	Exclude	Exclude	70	Exclude	5000	Max	Max	Max	Max	Max
53	Keurig Coffee Lovers' Collection...	Keurig	$32.24	Grocery & G...	#702	3,743	$120,674	3,699	4.5	2.4 lbs
65	LEVOIT Air Purifier for Home Al...	LEVOIT	$69.99	Home & Kit...	#2,033	3,499	$244,895	290	4.2	5 lbs
91	Dreaming Wapiti Pillows for Sle...	Dreaming Wapiti	$49.99	Home & Kit...	#1,036	4,996	$249,750	373	4.9	7.65 lbs

(Profit Miner — showing results for "-alkdjflakjdf")

After that, put in the maximum amount of reviews, which is 1,000 or less. (This keeps your competition lower.)

#	Product Name	Brand	Price	Category	Rank	Mo. Sales	Revenue	Reviews	Rating	Weight
Min	Include	Include	15	Include	300	Min	Min	Min	Min	Min
Max	Exclude	Exclude	70	Exclude	5000	Max	Max	1000	Max	Max
65	LEVOIT Air Purifier for Home Al...	LEVOIT	$69.99	Home & Kit...	#2,033	3,499	$244,895	290	4.2	5 lbs
91	Dreaming Wapiti Pillows for Sle...	Dreaming Wapiti	$49.99	Home & Kit...	#1,036	4,996	$249,750	373	4.9	7.65 lbs

(Profit Miner — showing results for "-alkdjflakjdf")

Next, enter five pounds for the maximum weight. This is important for your shipping costs. You want to keep your inventory shipments manageable as well.

Note: You might need to load more pages at this point to get more products to evaluate. I loaded an additional 5 pages because the final filter, weight, would have eliminated all remaining opportunities from the list.

#	Product Name	Brand	Price	Category	Rank	Mo. Sales	Revenue	Reviews	Rating	Weight
Min	Include	Include	15	Include	300	Min	Min	Min	Min	Min
Max	Exclude	Exclude	70	Exclude	5000	Max	Max	1000	Max	5
65	LEVOIT Air Purifier for Home Al...	LEVOIT	$69.99	Home & Kit...	#2,033	3,499	$244,895	290	4.2	5 lbs
AD	Pritom 7 inch Kids Tablet, Qua...	PRITOM	$59.99	Computers ...	#1,209	246	$14,758	32	3.2	1.65 lbs
AD	Fusion5 7" Android 8.1 Oreo Ta...	Fusion5	$59.97	Computers ...	#3,532	85	$5,097	168	3.2	0.88 lbs
155	MOOSOO Vacuum Cleaner Cor...	MOOSOO M	$59.99	Home & Kit...	#1,083	4,920	$295,151	705	4.1	3.3 lbs
AD	Pritom 7 inch Kids Tablet	Qua...	PRITOM	$59.99	Computers ...	#3,170	94	$5,639	8	3.2	1.63 lbs
205	Amazon Brand – 100 Ct. Solim...	Solimo	$26.08	Grocery & G...	#335	5,906	$154,028	33	4.3	3.6 lbs
216	Starbucks by Nespresso, Favori...	Starbucks by N...	$36.00	Grocery & G...	#310	6,148	$221,328	182	4.1	0.94 lbs

(Profit Miner — showing results for "-alkdjflakjdf")

As you can see, the product search is now showing only viable products based on the criteria I've inserted for a total of 240 products.

At this point, it's pretty easy to look through the results and see if a product interests you or not. If you're interested in a product, simply click on it, and you can see the full listing.

A great way to capture your results so you can continue to review and consider them is to download a spreadsheet of your search. In the bottom right hand corner you'll find a 'download' button, with the option of exporting to CSV. If you click on that and download, you will have an Excel sheet of all the products that matched your search criteria. From there, if you're interested in a product and want to research it further you can; if not, simply delete it from the file.

It's worth noting in the examples above that I only went through 10 pages. It's important that you take it further. You may not find anything in the first 10 pages that really interests you and also matches all five criteria. I highly encourage you to search deeper to find a product personal to you. Fortunately, the special product research extension enables you to do this quickly.

The last criteria for selecting a great product to sell is what we typically call "private label potential." Remember, to *make the most money* long-term, you want to create and own your own brand of products. You do *not* want to sell products with someone else's branding on them.

Fortunately, you can private label just about any product today. You only need to avoid highly complex products. For example, an iPhone or laptop computer are going to be very hard for you to private label and still sell a product with equal or better quality.

You're looking for basic, simple products with minimal branding. Soon you'll learn how to find suppliers for products. If you can find multiple suppliers offering generic versions of a product, chances are you can private label it.

If you're concerned about any patent issues with the product you find, it's a good idea to do a patent search online or talk with an attorney.

HOW BART VAN IERSEL-DE JONG ESCAPED CORPORATE LIFE BY SELLING A PRIVATE-LABEL PRODUCT.

Bart van Iersel - De Jong knew corporate life wasn't for him.

Living in the Netherlands with his partner Elke and their baby girl, he dreamed of a different lifestyle. "Freedom and connection with family are very important to me. I hated going out to work leaving Elke at home, and having no choice in that matter. I set a strong goal to change this — to become more free."

So, in 2013, Bart and Elke decided to give the business model you're learning about in this book a try. Their first product wasn't perfect, but it gave them a start.

"We picked a very niche product: resin fairy houses to put in miniature gardens... I later learned the market of these products is way too small," says Bart. Nonetheless, the houses started selling and Bart and Elke continued to add products. By March 2014, they were selling $14,000 per month from 40 different products.

"That was the moment that it clicked in my brain," Bart recalls. "[I realized] this Amazon business is no joke; this can replace my job."

Through our training, Bart learned that they needed to select a different product if they really wanted to grow. So they tried again. "This time, we picked the right product: a big enough market, and good private label potential. Our goal was to replace the revenue from the fairy houses with a single private label product. We picked a product, and successfully found a supplier. That product went off to do $15,000 in monthly revenue just like we hoped."

By December 2014 Elke and Bart had another child on the way, and Bart was still juggling their Amazon business with his regular job. Despite their busy schedules, "we were dreaming big, visualizing our goals of freedom and wealth."

And then Bart lost his job. While many people would have considered this a crisis, Bart and Elke saw it as an opportunity.

"Through a huge synergistic and lucky event, my employer decided to fire me. It was true, even though I put in my best efforts, corporate life wasn't for me. This turned out to be a huge blessing, and a resounding answer to our dreams. The [termination] agreement allowed us some financial security for a few more months — exactly what we needed to make the business grow further."

Bart and Elke turned their full efforts towards launching their second product and sourcing five more. "Our goal was clear: grow to a size where the business supports our lifestyle twice over. Over 2015 we grew a lot, and by 2016 we achieved a 7-figure revenue per year. Today we sell over 20 products, still in the 7-figure per year revenue range."

"Since then we've had many amazing experiences like living in a mansion, employing a private butler, buying our dream car, traveling, and growing our family to now have four lovely daughters."

Bart acknowledges that it hasn't been easy. "We've experienced a lot of ups and downs over the years, but every time [we've had a setback] we have recovered and grown the business. We've also gone through a huge spiritual journey together, growing immensely as people and getting increasingly clear on what is important for us in our life."

Corporate life is now a distant memory for Bart. "We are still free from the 9-to-5, empowered to make our own choices in how we want to live our life, and how and where we want to work. I mostly work from home so I'm very close to my family. Honestly, I can't imagine having to go back to a job."

Quick re-cap and what's up next...

In this chapter you learned about the five critical criteria for choosing a great product. You learned about BSR—an important piece of information that will ensure you choose a product that people are already buying. And you learned exactly how to find a great product opportunity on Amazon.

In the next chapter, I'll show you how to find suppliers who are eager to work with you. You'll learn the simple steps to turn one of the opportunities you find on Amazon into a real, live product with your own branding on it! This information is important because knowing how to find opportunities isn't enough—you need to know how to find the highest quality suppliers and how to negotiate for the best pricing and terms in order to build a profitable business. You'll also learn how to run your business with no warehouse, no order handling, no website, and no staff.

Your life changes once you have a brand you own, selling a product that's yours, producing profit for you each and every day—even while you sleep! You break the cycle of trading time for money and get on the path to financial freedom. The sooner you start, the sooner you can be free.

YOUR NEXT ACTION: FIND A PRODUCT OPPORTUNITY.

Before you continue reading, take action right now. Go find a product opportunity with the instructions you've just read about.

Remember, you can get your product research extension here: **www.MillionDollarBrandBook.com/finder**

You don't have to get it perfect. Just start.

BUILD A BUSINESS THAT WORKS FOR YOU:

HOW TO FIND HIGH-QUALITY SUPPLIERS AND NEARLY AUTOMATE YOUR ENTIRE BUSINESS.

03

How many vacation days have you used this year?

According to a recent survey, the majority of people are afraid to take a vacation. They fear they'll get fired or will get behind on work.

That is no way to live.

You *can* control your own schedule, choose when to work, work from anywhere in the world, and decide how much money you make. You *can* travel, go on adventures, spend time with your family, enjoy life, and help those you care about.

To do this, you need a business that works for you. You need to own a business that produces income for you around the clock, whether you're working or not. In this chapter, you'll learn how to build exactly that.

To start, you need to find a good product opportunity. Amazon, the world's largest retailer, gives you this information right at your fingertips—*if* you know where to look.

As you learned in the last chapter, you start by finding a product with high sales and low competition that meets five specific criteria. Any product you choose should:

- Be ranked between 300-5000 on Amazon
- Sell for between $15 to $70
- Have fewer than 1,000 reviews
- Be something you can brand / private label
- Weigh less than five pounds

In this chapter you'll learn how to find a high-quality supplier for any product you want to sell. Plus, you'll learn how to run this business from anywhere in the world with just a laptop and an internet connection.

YOUR STEPS WILL BE AS FOLLOWS:

Step 1: Establish a brand for the products you're about to sell.

In 2010, a year after I started my ecommerce business, sales were taking off. I'd figured out online advertising and was driving thousands of dollars in sales every day of products I sold that were created by other brands.

But there were some big problems. My competitors selling the same branded products were upset I was advertising online, running promotional discounts, and selling places they didn't understand, like Amazon. They complained to the brand owners constantly. Each day, I'd have five or more emails from the owners of the brands I was selling telling me what I could and could not do selling *their* products.

Plus, I was settling for a lower profit margin because the brand owner was usually just a middleman between me and the real manufacturer.

A couple years in, I figured out how to "private label" the exact same products these brands were selling. My costs for these products went down by 70%, resulting in a much higher profit margin. Also, for once, I controlled the brand and could sell *my* products however I wanted.

This experience changed everything for me and is what we at Amazing have been showing people ever since.

STEP 1 Establish a brand for the products you're about to sell.

STEP 2 Find a manufacturer that can put your brand name and logo on a product.

STEP 3 Calculate your profit margin.

STEP 4 Verify the quality of the products you wish to sell.

STEP 5 Order your inventory.

STEP 6 Contact a freight forwarder.

To make the most money and have the most control, you must own the brand. It's simpler than it sounds. You just need a logo and a brand name. You can get a logo designed online on a website such as Fiverr.com for as little as $10. For your brand name, you just need something short and memorable that fits the market and the products you want to sell.

To help you do this, I've put together a **Brand Creation Checklist** for you. Use this simple checklist to build your new brand.

THE BRAND CREATION CHECKLIST

When it comes down to it, a brand is simply a name—but there are steps you need to follow to create a good one. Picking a name at random without any thought is not going to work, but it also doesn't have to be a complicated process.

There are only three steps to follow:

 1 CHOOSE YOUR BRAND NAME   **2** CREATE YOUR LOGO    **3** CREATE YOUR BRAND ASSETS

CHOOSE YOUR BRAND NAME

1. **Your brand name should be related to the market in which you are selling (especially the demographic)**

   Example: Fitness-related brand:
   - Golden Age Athletics (older demographic)
   - Elite Athletics (professional/advanced demographic)

2. **Your brand name should not restrict your choice of future products**

   Example: Yoga brand:
   - Yoga for You
   - Bare Movement

   The latter brand name gives you a much broader scope for the future should you expand beyond yoga.

3. **Ensure that your brand name passes the "phone test"**

   Example: Smart Solutions is much easier than Ingenious Solutions

- Make sure it is easy to spell, pronounce, and remember
- Could a friend or family member talking to you on the phone clearly understand and spell your brand name after hearing you say it? If not, try a different name.

4. Make sure that your brand name is available

- Go to the USPTO trademark database (www.uspto.gov)
- Use the Basic Word Mark Search to make sure the brand name you want has not been trademarked

5. Make sure that your brand name domain is available

- Go to www.namecheap.com and enter your brand name without any spaces or punctuation
- Make sure the .com domain is available

If it passes all the tests, congratulations, you have your brand name!

CREATE YOUR LOGO

1. A designer does most of the work for you, but you must provide them with:

- Your preferred color scheme
- Directions on the look and feel (edgy, professional, youthful, refined, etc.)
- An idea of what your market might respond to—if you're not sure, look at other brands in your market and check out their logos

2. Make sure you follow these guidelines when designing a logo:

- It should be easy to read and recognize
- It must work well on both a dark and a light background
- Simpler is better (the Apple logo is a great example of a simple, easily recognizable logo)

Trust your designer and make sure you get their input on your ideas — remember that they are the professional.

3. Where to Get Your Logo Designed

There are many places where you can get your logo designed, but we recommend the following, as they work whether you have a small or a large design budget:

- **Fiverr:** Providers on this site offer all kinds of services (or "gigs").
  - » Logo design = $5 to $20
  - » The good: Fast and cheap
  - » The not so good: Not the highest quality, and you can only use one designer per gig

- **99 Designs:** Post a job on this site, and designers submit their designs.
  - » Cost: $299+
  - » The good: Higher quality and a large number of designs
  - » The not so good: More expensive and can be slower (5-7 days)

CREATE YOUR BRAND ASSETS

1. Brand Asset #1 (required): Brand Website
- Can be simple; no need for a complicated website. (Use Wix, Squarespace, or Wordpress for instance.)
- They all contain drag and drop builders
- No web design experience required
- Include your brand name and logo on main page

2. Brand Asset #2 (required): Facebook Brand Page
- The process is very straightforward
- Facebook has made it a very easy step-by-step process
- Go to https://www.facebook.com/pages/creation/
- Start with the Brand or Website option

3. Other Brand Assets You Can Create (not required)
- Instagram account
- Twitter account
- Pinterest account
- Google account (for Google Advertising)

Follow all the steps in this guide and you will have your very own brand!

Step 2: Find a manufacturer that can put your brand name and logo on a product.

To find a manufacturer that can put your brand name and logo on a product similar to what you find on Amazon, you only need two resources: Google and Alibaba.

First, you need to decide whether you want to work with a manufacturer in the US or internationally. If you're looking for a manufacturer of a nutritional supplement or a beauty product you put on your body, you're likely going to want a US-based manufacturer.

Here's how to find a US manufacturer.

To find a US manufacturer, you just need to do a quick Google search. To do that, all you do is type in the kind of product you are looking for, add the phrase "private label", and search. It's really that simple.

For example, to find a manufacturer to make probiotics, simply search for "probiotics private label". Doing this returned nearly 694,000 results within seconds.

Now, not *all* of these are private label suppliers. However, many of them are and are looking for sellers just like you and me to supply products to.

All you need to do is click on a few, check out what they have to offer, and then contact them to get pricing and their minimum order requirements.

When I click on the supplier shown in the example below, I can see that they offer multiple types of private label probiotic blends and are looking for sellers like us who want to create their own branded versions of these products.

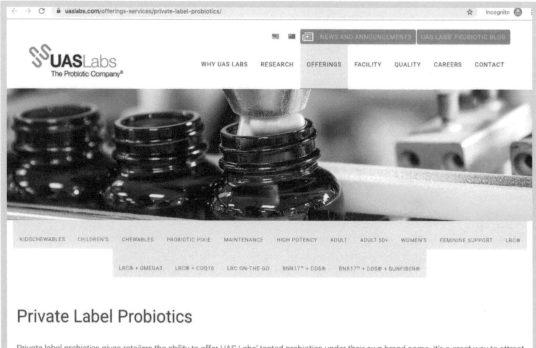

To get in touch with this manufacturer, I'd simply look for the instructions to contact them and use the supplier contact template that you'll find at the end of this chapter to get their pricing, options, and terms.

It's best to contact at least three different suppliers to get different quotes. As you go, be sure and keep track of everyone you contacted so you can compare them later on.

What if the product you want to sell is manufactured in China or another country outside the US?

China is the leading country in the world for manufacturing output. Chances are, the product you want to create your own brand of is manufactured primarily in China.

Today, finding a supplier in China, or just about anywhere outside the US, is simple. Use the website Alibaba.com. Alibaba is one of the largest companies in the world based out of China and traded on the New York Stock Exchange. With this site, you can find and connect with manufacturers all over the world, not just in China.

One question we get a lot is, "How do I avoid getting low-quality products from bad manufacturers in China?" What a lot of people fail to realize is that some of the very highest quality, best known products are manufactured in China, including the Apple iPhone.

As with any country, including the US, there are high-quality manufacturers with great products and low-quality manufacturers with bad products. With the process you'll learn shortly, you'll order samples of the actual product you'll be selling from multiple manufacturers. By doing this, you'll make sure you sell a great, high-quality product you're proud of.

Here's how to find a supplier using Alibaba: First, head to alibaba.com. Locate the search box, and type in the name of the product. In the example below, I've used "wireless barcode scanner."

Once you've typed in your product name, click on Search. As you can see in the example above, this generates a lot of results — 14,652 for this one product. But don't worry, you can narrow that down quickly by supplier location.

For most products, you'll likely choose China as your supplier location, but you can check the other boxes too. To keep it simple in this example, I've only selected China. (Note: it will allow you to pick specific areas in China. Don't do that—it's far too restrictive.)

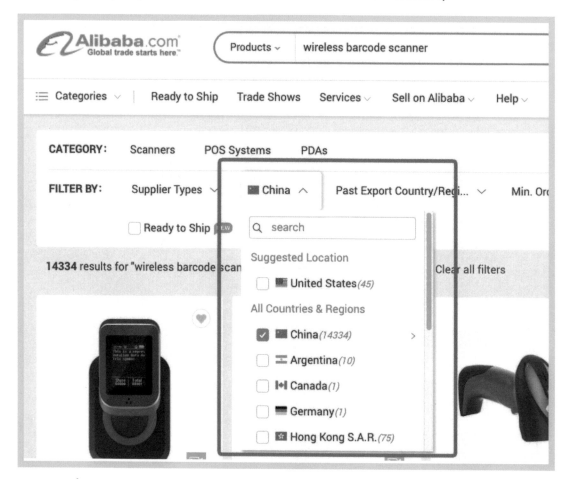

REMINDER: DO WHAT YOU SAY YOU WILL DO.

Being true to your word, and being a trustworthy, reliable, decent person to work with, is essential in this business—and any other.

If you try to get ahead by cutting corners, taking advantage of other people, or falling through on your commitments, you will destroy your chances of success long-term.

Do what you say you will do. Treat your suppliers, customers, partners, vendors, and everyone you do business with like you would a close, lifelong friend. Act honestly, do right by others, and, in the long-run, you'll reap the rewards.

Treat people well and you'll be more successful, experience less stress, and have a lot more fun on your way to a great life!

Next, click on 'Supplier Types' and check the box for 'Trade Assurance.' Choosing this box means the supplier supports Trade Assurance—a free service that protects your orders from payment to delivery. In other words, it ensures that the supplier can't change any of the terms once you've agreed to them.

After that, go back to the 'Supplier Types' filter. This time, check the box for 'Verified Supplier.' This refers to a premium membership for higher level suppliers. By checking this box, you rule out a lot of the smaller suppliers and looking for only the best and biggest suppliers.

With that done, the results have been narrowed down from 14,000 to less than 4,000. While that is still a huge number of results, you don't need to go through them all.

Once you have your results, you can start looking at the individual product listings from suppliers. Click on the ones that most resemble the product you want to sell based on what you found on Amazon.

As you go through each of the listings, you'll review several pieces of information. The first is the price. In some cases, the suppliers will show you the minimum order along with the price. This is known as minimum order quantity, or MOQ. You want to find a low minimum order quantity, and a low price. Importantly, the information on these listings is only a baseline and may not be 100% accurate. Just because it says $18 it doesn't mean it's going to be $18; you will only get the true price and the true MOQ by contacting suppliers and working with them.

It's critically important to build a relationship with your supplier. You can't just send them one question and forget about it. You need to interact with them, and be willing to message them back and forth. (As you'll see, we've created a supplier contact template to help you with this.)

To contact a supplier on Alibaba, start by opening one of the listings. Next, just click on the image or link of the item listing you wish to view and it will open the actual listing for the product where it will give you more information.

In the above example, the supplier is giving prices for various quantities ordered. The price for between 2-9 units is $17.90 each. If you order more than 100 units, the price is $15.90 each.

If you contact the supplier, you can typically get much larger discounts for ordering more units at a time.

You can also dig a little further on Alibaba. You'll often find nearly identical products for far cheaper. For example, this barcode scanner is listed for as low as $11.00 per unit:

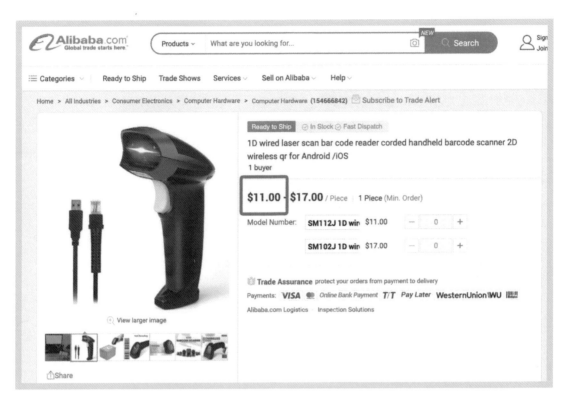

Once you've opened up a listing, click on 'Contact Supplier'. It will then open up a contact box. That's where you write your message to contact the supplier.

Your objective is to contact at least ten suppliers. You need to contact multiple suppliers because you want to find the best quality product you can, the best MOQ, and the best price.

As you'll see in the template I've provided below, you need to ask suppliers about MOQ, price, lead time, and how long it takes for them to create the product. Once you get information from ten different suppliers you can start assessing which ones you prefer. At that point, if you have two or three suppliers you like, continue with the process by asking more questions.

Don't let contacting suppliers intimidate you. It's a straightforward process thousands of people with the same or less experience as you have successfully navigated. Be patient and persistent and you will find the perfect supplier for your product.

If you ever have any communication issues with suppliers, don't worry. This is normal. There are periods throughout the year, such as during Chinese New Year, suppliers may be less responsive.

If you make sure to look for the appropriate criteria on Alibaba and order samples, you should be able to find a good supplier for your product.

One additional factor to consider when evaluating suppliers, is their communication quality and speed. Some suppliers are much easier to work with than others with equivalent product quality. How they communicate with you during your initial communications is a good indicator of how future communications will be with them. Take note of this for each supplier and factor it into your ultimate decision of which supplier you choose.

SUPPLIER CONTACT TEMPLATE

Use these templates to guide you as you start reaching out to your suppliers. Do not copy them word-for-word. Use them as inspiration, and make them your own!

SUPPLIER TEMPLATE #1

Dear [Contact Name and Manufacturer]:

My name is [your full name] and I am the owner of [company or brand name], a company specializing in products for [insert your industry or area of interest here]. We are currently looking to expand our product line and are interested in one of the items that you manufacture, the [insert product name here and link as well].

Can you please provide me with the following additional information so that we can determine if this is a good fit for our product line?

- Are you able to provide custom packaging?
- What is the standard production time for each order?
- What is the price per unit (including packaging) at the following MOQs:
    » 100 to 500 pcs:
    » 501 to 1000 pcs:
    » 1001 to 5000 pcs:
    » 5001 and higher pcs:

I appreciate your time and look forward to hearing from you soon so that we can move forward with our next order.

Sincerely,
Name, Title
Company or Brand

Dear Sara Wang, Yangho Cosmetics Company:

My name is Bob Smith and I am the owner of RL Smith Cosmetics, a company specializing in products for the beauty industry. We are currently looking to expand our product line and are interested in one of the items that you manufacture, the 10 piece set of beauty brushes.

Can you please provide me with the following additional information so that we can determine if this is a good fit for our product line?

- Are you able to provide custom packaging?
- What is the standard production time for each order?
- What is the price per unit (including packaging) at the following MOQs:
  - » 100 to 500 pcs:
  - » 501 to 1000 pcs:
  - » 1001 to 5000 pcs:
  - » 5001 and higher pcs:

I appreciate your time and look forward to hearing from you soon, so that we can move forward with our next order.

Sincerely,
Bob Smith, Owner
RL Smith Cosmetics

Step 3: Calculate your profit margin.

The system I just showed you works because each party gets to specialize in what they do best: Amazon specializes in offering a massive marketplace with millions of products, your manufacturer specializes in manufacturing the product and selling it in bulk to brand owners, and you specialize in building a brand and selling your products directly to consumers.

You see, manufacturers *need* people like you and me. They'll be competing for your business to supply products for your brand because that is how they make money.

This type of physical products business can be incredibly profitable—just look at one of the biggest companies in the world, Apple, which has hundreds of billions of dollars in cash generated at its disposal.

With a physical products business, you're selling products people want and need in their lives. It's a highly scalable, sustainable, profitable business that will always exist.

But in order to maximize your profits you need to understand what a good profit margin is and how to calculate it.

FAQ: WHAT ARE THE PROS AND CONS OF WORKING WITH AN AMERICAN SUPPLIER VS AN INTERNATIONAL SUPPLIER?

Health supplements and beauty products like creams and oils are typically manufactured in the USA due to quality standards and legal restrictions. Just about anything else will be made overseas, typically in China.

Here are some of the advantages and disadvantages of working with American vs International suppliers.

- **Advantages of selling products made in the US:**
  - » Faster production time typically
  - » Easier communication
  - » Sometimes lower cost per unit and lower minimum order quantity (MOQ)

- **Disadvantages of selling products made in the US:**
  - » Fewer products to choose from
  - » More competition
  - » Regulation/liability around supplements and beauty products

- **Advantages of selling products made in China:**
  - » More products to choose from
  - » Less competition for many of the products than typical supplements & beauty products

- **Disadvantages of selling products made in China:**
  - » Longer lead time
  - » Potential communication issues

To calculate a product's profit potential, there are only a few pieces of information you need to get:

- The cost of the product
- The price that you will be selling it for
- Any fees Amazon charges in order to leverage their incredible platform full of customers and for their fulfilment services

To get the cost of the product, simply look at the prices you found when doing your product research for a supplier. On Alibaba, most suppliers give you a price range that depends on how many you order. You'll most likely pay something towards the higher end of that range for your first order. But as you grow your business and order more, you'll pay less and scale your profits even higher.

I recommend estimating the price somewhere in the middle of the range to begin with. With time and increased sales, your product cost per unit will decrease. But, estimating a slightly higher product cost per unit in the beginning helps take into account any other costs you might have to pay, such as increased tariffs and shipping.

If the supplier doesn't have the pricing listed, no problem—you can use the Supplier Contact Template provided earlier to get the information you need.

Once you have the product cost, you then need to decide the selling price for your product. Since you have modeled your product after one that you found on Amazon using the specific criteria you learned about in Chapter 2, the best price to use as an estimated selling price is the same price similar products sell for on Amazon.

A common mistake is to assume you'll be able to charge more initially for your new product. Eventually, you may be able to; however, you want to make sure the product you choose can be profitable selling at a price similar to the products like yours already selling on Amazon.

This doesn't mean that you'll always sell at that price. As a matter of fact, it's wise to initially price your product a little lower than the competition as you build up your sales. The goal will be to get up to their price, or maybe even higher, so this is a good safe number to use as your target.

The last piece of information you need to know is what types of fees Amazon will take every time you make a sale on their site. While Amazon outlines these fees in great detail inside your Seller account, the easiest way to see them is to use something called the FBA Revenue Calculator Tool.

You can find this tool with a quick Google search:

Google   fba revenue calculator   🎤   🔍

🔍 All   ▶ Videos   ◇ Shopping   🗒 News   🖼 Images   ⋮ More   Settings   Tools

About 207,000 results (0.68 seconds)

FBA Revenue Calculator - Amazon Seller Central
https://sellercentral.amazon.com › fba › profitabilitycalculator ▾
No information is available for this page.
Learn why

Open this webpage and I'll walk you through using Amazon's FBA Revenue Calculator step-by-step.

The first step is to put in the ASIN of the product you found on Amazon. The ASIN is the Amazon Standard Identification Number. It's a 10-character identifier assigned by Amazon, which you can find on any product listing page on Amazon, as shown here:

Additional Information

ASIN	B01GDJ2BH6
Customer Reviews	☆☆☆☆☆ ˅ 402 customer reviews 4.4 out of 5 stars
Best Sellers Rank	#1,033 in Office Products (See Top 100 in Office Products) #1 in Bar Code Scanners
Shipping Weight	11.2 ounces (View shipping rates and policies)
Date First Available	May 31, 2016

Enter the ASIN from the product you found on Amazon into the FBA Revenue Calculator tool:

amazon services
seller central

Fulfillment by Amazon Revenue Calculator
Provide your fulfillment costs and see real-time cost comparisons bet

Disclaimer The Fulfilment by Amazon Revenue Calculator should be used as a guide in eval Calculator should be conducted to verify the results. Fulfilment by Amazon Revenue Calculat subject to separate rates. Refer to the FBA Pricing page for up-to-date costs and fees.

Find your product on Amazon.com

B01GDJ2BH6
Search

> **You see, manufacturers need people like you and me. They'll be competing for your business to supply products for your brand because that is how they make money.**

Next, enter the price that you plan on selling it for in the Amazon Fulfillment column. You're using this column because, if you follow our recommended instructions, Amazon will take care of shipping orders and storing inventory for you. In this example, I'm using the same price the product is selling for on Amazon: $34.99.

It's a good idea to take into account any shipping costs to get this product all the way from the manufacturer to Amazon. I recommend estimating this cost at about $1.00 per unit. It may end up being slightly more or less, but this is a good estimate to use when starting out.

The last number to enter is your cost estimate for your product. Remember to use a product cost price in the middle of the range from Alibaba. Or, if you've received pricing information directly from a supplier, you can use that instead. In this example, I chose $13.00 (Alibaba showed a price range of $11.00-$17.00). When you've entered your numbers, hit the Calculate button.

The calculator tool takes into account all of Amazon's fees, including storing and shipping the product to customers. You can see that this product can make a profit of over 41%, or $14.66, per unit sold.

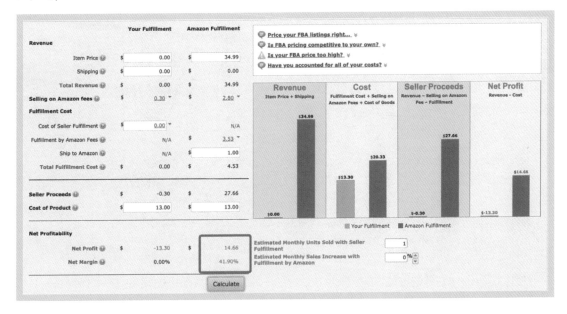

We recommend a profit margin of 25-40%. Some sellers have higher profit margins than this, which is great. But, with a profit margin in this range, you can advertise your product and reinvest a portion of profits back in your business. As a result, you'll be able to scale your business as fast as possible.

Step 4: Verify the quality of the products you wish to sell.

Once you've found a supplier and verified a good potential profit margin, it's time to verify the product quality. You accomplish this by ordering a product sample from the supplier. We typically recommend ordering a sample from three different suppliers so you can compare the quality of the product and communications.

Usually, a supplier will charge you $50-$60 for the sample, which includes shipping. The sample can typically be shipped to anywhere in the world.

When you receive the product sample, you should use test out the product yourself. Assess the quality and durability of the product as much as possible. If you can, get a friend or family member who could be a potential customer for the product to use the sample and give you feedback. It's important to build your business around a product your customers will be happy with.

Once you've verified the quality of the product sample and have created your brand name and logo, you're ready to order your first shipment of inventory! This exciting time means your business is about to come to life. Soon, you'll have a product you can touch and hold and show to others that you created with your own brand name on it.

HOW MICHAEL SHINNICK MADE INTERNATIONAL SUPPLIERS THE KEY TO HIS SUCCESS.

Michael Shinnick knows the difference between a smart business model and an unstable one. As a Business and Executive Coach in Dublin, Ireland, he wanted to apply his expertise to a venture of his own. But when he started looking for a new business opportunity, he was generally disappointed in what he saw.

After looking at various possibilities, including other online business models, "they didn't seem to be that well thought out. They had no structure or process."

So when a fellow business advisor raved about Amazing Selling Machine, Michael decided to check it out. He was pleasantly surprised. "The professional nature of their training structure was so different from anything else I had come across."

The business model proved to be more than highly profitable. Michael now has one brand and about 30 SKUs in the US and Europe. His annual revenue is $1.8 million, with an average gross profit margin of 42%.

"The business is very profitable and a great source of income," reflects Michael. "I love the fact that I am building a brand and creating it from scratch. Very few other business models would enable you to do this so quickly."

The secret to Michael's amazing results? He says that finding the right suppliers has been instrumental to his success... and one of the surprising benefits of the business.

"Tracking down and negotiating with a supplier was a key part to my success. I sourced my first supplier through the Alibaba site using the scripts from Amazing. I contacted quite a few, requesting quotations. If these quotations were acceptable I then looked for samples and narrowed it down from there. I now mainly find suppliers in trade shows like the Global Sources Electronics Show and the HKTDC Electronics show in Hong Kong. I have also travelled to the Yiwu Market in China and plan on going to the Canton Fair in the near future."

While meeting your suppliers in person certainly isn't essential, Michael values the opportunity to do so. "As my business and product range grew I found meeting my suppliers as well as going to trade shows and fairs in Hong Kong and China to be very useful. [I love that] the business affords me the opportunity to travel the world to meet my suppliers, attend trade shows, and to mingle with other great e-commerce sellers at conferences and masterminds."

Meanwhile, he's discovered a wealth of opportunity for expansion. "There are almost infinite opportunities to expand our range of SKUs in the Consumer Electronics arena."

Michael's advice—much like he would teach his coaching clients, no doubt— is to "commit to making a success of the business. Invest in the knowledge and processes and follow [the ASM] system to the letter at the beginning. Take your time researching the right products and finding the best suppliers. The time taken here will repay you in the future. But most importantly, get started and commit to its success."

Step 5: Order your inventory.

When you're ready, contact the supplier and tell them how many units you want to order. They'll give you a quote and if you're happy with it, you can place your initial inventory order.

Typically, the manufacturer will require a 30% down payment before they start manufacturing your product. The other 70% is due when the product is ready to ship.

When you're buying inventory, you're purchasing an asset. For example, if you buy 500 units at $5 each with shipping, that's a $2,500 investment. If you're able to sell that inventory after all costs and fees for $5,000, then you've doubled your initial investment. The faster you get your product live and repeat the cycle of investing in inventory and selling it, the more money you make.

Step 6: Contact a freight forwarder.

When I first started my ecommerce business, I didn't have anyone to teach me. So, I learned a lot of stuff the hard way. I sold on my own websites, which meant I had to manage the hosting account, deal with payment processors, process refunds and chargebacks, and deal with fraudulent orders which popped up every year around Black Friday and other big shopping times.

I even had a small warehouse where I kept and shipped out hundreds of packages every single day—where usually an employee or myself, and sometimes even my soon-to-be wife stuffed products into envelopes frantically before USPS came to pick them up at the end of the day.

Luckily, you can learn from my mistakes. You can build and grow your business as big as you want from anywhere in the world with just a laptop and an internet connection. You can manage your business while traveling with your family or hanging out on a beach in Thailand if you wish. You can work from home—and never have to go into an office again—for the rest of your life once your business is up and running. And you can do it without adding stress to your dating life by making your significant other stuff envelopes on date night...

Here's how you can build a physical products business without ever touching any inventory yourself.

Once you've found the product you want to sell, order inventory from a manufacturer.

When that batch of inventory is ready, contact what's called a "freight forwarder" to arrange shipment from the manufacturer all the way to Amazon. These specialized companies make their money from handling the logistics of getting your inventory from your manufacturer to where you need it to go - Amazon's FBA warehouses, in this case. Freight forwarder costs are typically very reasonable. To get the best pricing, it's always a good idea to get quotes from at least two different freight forwarders, especially for your first shipment. If your inventory is coming from overseas, use a freight forwarder to make your life easier.

REMEMBER:

Financial success requires investment. Know that when you're buying inventory, you're planting seeds that can make money for you in the future.

They'll contact the supplier, pick up the inventory, get it all the way from the supplier to where you're going to sell it, inspect it, and ship it to Amazon.

For example, if your manufacturer is in China and you're selling on Amazon.com in the U.S., the freight forwarder will arrange to pick up the inventory from the manufacturer's warehouse, transport it to the local port, ship it by sea across the ocean, pick it up at the port in the U.S., transport it to the freight forwarder's warehouse, inspect the inventory, and lastly ship it to Amazon.

Once your inventory is with Amazon, you're ready to start selling!

When a customer buys from you on Amazon, Amazon will automatically take care of picking, packing, and shipping the order to the customer—you don't have to do anything. Amazon even takes care of all the returns and refunds for you.

This system is called Fulfillment by Amazon, or FBA. With it, your products are automatically Prime-eligible for free two-day shipping. In fact, Amazon recently invested $800 million to make Prime shipping even faster, aiming to make one-day deliveries available to everyone. Using FBA as an Amazon seller, you get the full benefits of this massive investment.

Every day, Amazon will automatically process sales on its website for your product and ship out orders to customers. Every two weeks, Amazon will send a payment to your bank account for the sales you've made.

Once your inventory starts to run low, you simply contact your supplier again and have them prepare more inventory. When the new batch of inventory is ready, contact your freight forwarder and repeat the process.

The result of your efforts? Imagine being on a relaxing vacation with your family. You have a few extra minutes, so you login to your Amazon Seller Central account to check out your stats for the day. You notice you've sold 20 units so far at a profit of $15 each. Amazon is preparing the shipments. You don't have to do anything. While you've been doing what you want with those you love, your business has made you $300 wealthier. This is the reward of owning your own business using this efficient model.

Let's pause here for a moment and review what you've learned so far.

In Chapter 1, you learned about the incredible opportunity to build a business today, especially an ecommerce business. Online retail is making up more and more of total retail each year. It's continuing to grow at an incredible rate. By building your own ecommerce business today, you can build a business much faster and easier than if you wait months or years to start.

You also learned about the importance of selling a great product. You want a high-quality product that your customers love. Fortunately, today this is easier than ever. You simply need to seek out a good product opportunity leveraging the information available on Amazon.

As you learned in Chapter 2, you're looking for product opportunities that meet five criteria: can sell for $15 to $70; has less than 1,000 reviews; is ranked 300 to 5,000 on Amazon; weighs less than five pounds; and can be private labeled.

In Chapter 3, you learned the value of owning your own brand—and how easy it is to create one. I showed you how to find suppliers in the US using simple Google searches and how to find suppliers in China and beyond without ever having to take one step outside your house using Alibaba.

Lastly, you learned that as long as you have a laptop and an internet connection, you can build and run this business from anywhere in the world. Your supplier prepares your inventory, a freight forwarder gets your inventory to Amazon, Amazon prepares and ships orders to the people who buy from you, and you get paid every two weeks directly to your bank account!

In the next chapter, you'll learn how to leverage the power of Facebook's two billion users to build a list of people eager to buy your new product. You'll also learn how to target Amazon's 100 million Prime members with a brand new marketing tool recently released. You are among the first to see these new marketing strategies to grow sales for a brand new product on Amazon!

YOUR NEXT ACTION: FIND AND CONTACT A SUPPLIER.

Time to start applying what you learned in this chapter: Use the steps you just read about to find at least one supplier for the product opportunity you discovered in the previous chapter.

To help you with this, I've created a pre-written message you can copy and paste. Use the **Supplier Contact Template** provided earlier in this chapter to send a supplier a message.

Remember, you committed to using this information to change your life. The more action you take, the closer you get to the freedom you want. Give the instructions you read a try and see what happens; you have nothing to lose and everything to gain.

Don't wait. Start now.

BEAT BIG BRANDS ON AMAZON: HOW YOUR BRAND THAT "NO ONE'S EVER HEARD OF" CAN OUT-SELL THE BIG GUYS.

Have you ever bought a product on Amazon?

If your answer is "yes" (and I'm pretty sure that it is) you know how easy it is to search for a product to buy. You simply use Amazon's "search" function. Specifically, you click on the search bar at the top of the page and type in what you're looking for. Then you look at the results Amazon shows you and pick the one that looks the best. This is how everybody uses Amazon, which receives two billion visits per month!

So, if you want to make a lot of money, wouldn't it be valuable to know how to get your product to show up for the most popular keywords people are searching for?

That's what this chapter is all about. You'll learn brand new strategies to get a product you own to rank near the top for high-value search terms on Amazon. With this knowledge, you'll be able to beat big brands and make sales on the world's largest ecommerce store.

Soon, people will search on Amazon and find your product. When they buy it, you make money. You'll have a cash-producing business that you can run from anywhere in the world with just a laptop.

In this chapter, you'll learn powerful strategies to sell your product, including:

- How to use keywords to increase sales of your product
- How to use product listing optimization
- Marketing strategies to push your product up in the rankings for high-value keywords

All these strategies work together to ensure eager buyers discover and purchase your product.

Following these steps will help ensure your products are discovered by the right customer.

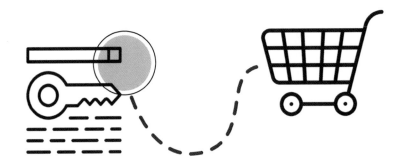

How to sell your products—even when nobody knows your brand.

One of the most common questions we get is, "How can I make sales with my new brand no one has ever heard of?"

Here's the answer.

Millions of shoppers use Amazon's search box to find products. To make sales as a product owner, you simply need to get *your* product to show up near the top of the search results pages. (You can probably guess how important this is based on your own online shopping experience. Most of us don't scroll beyond the first couple of pages before deciding what product to buy.)

So how do you get your product to come up in search? First, you need to know which relevant keywords to target. There are millions of different search terms people use. Most products only target 1-2 of the most popular keywords, but you can build a lot of sales momentum by targeting some of the lesser-known keywords. Later on, you can go after more competitive keywords as your product has more good reviews on Amazon. Sound counter-intuitive? Let me explain.

Imagine you're a store owner and you're looking to purchase a barcode scanner for your business. Since Amazon has become a top place for business owners to shop, you head on over and begin your search for the perfect scanner.

Now most people would simply type in "barcode scanner". As you can see, that pulls up a lot of results...over 3,000 of them.

Even though most people search with broad search terms like "barcode scanner", many people choose to use more specific search phrases to find the exact product they're looking for. Amazon knows this, so when you search you'll see a list of popular searches people use when narrowing down their list of products.

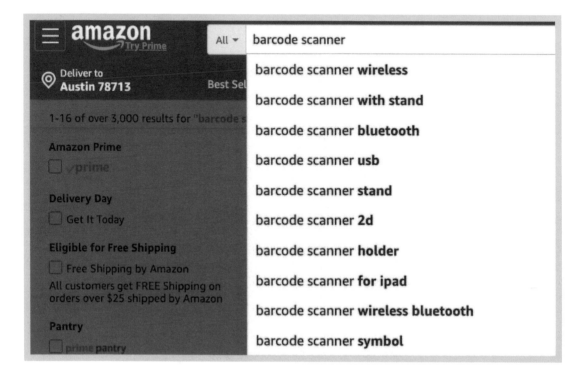

Suppose, in this example, you've decided you want not just a barcode scanner, but a *wireless* barcode scanner. So you do that search.

This time, the number of results has dropped drastically—from 3,000 to 956.

Now suppose you realize, by looking at Amazon's suggestions again, that you want to be able to read QR codes... so you make your search even more specific.

At that point you have a much more manageable list of just under 300 products.

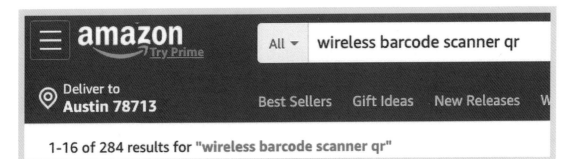

As a seller, this is exactly the type of keyword that you should focus on. To compete with only 300 products out of the 3 billion on Amazon will make it much easier to rank highly and start getting sales quickly.

Even though you may start off focusing on these more specific, less common keywords, as soon as you start making sales your product will begin ranking for more broad, more popular related keywords. (In the example I've been using, this means in time you would rank for searches such as "wireless barcode scanner" and even "barcode scanner" itself.) By starting with these less competitive search terms, you'll have an advantage over everyone else who naively focus on only the most competitive ones.

How to create a highly optimized product listing.

We've spent the past eight years analyzing how Amazon's algorithm ranks products for keywords, like the examples I just gave you. Much of it stays the same, but it's constantly evolving. The primary factor is how well your product page converts visitors into buyers. Amazon wants to make more money, so it features products that convert more visitors into buyers closer to the top of search results pages.

That means the first step in making sales on Amazon is to make sure you have a product listing that does the best job possible to convince people to *buy*.

To build a good product listing, you need to focus on four key parts of your listing:

- Your title
- Your pictures
- Your bullet points & description
- "Back-end search terms" (I'll explain this shortly)

Part 1. Choosing your title

After years of studying how Amazon works, we've found there is one must-have tactic that will help get your product ranked near the top of search results pages more than anything else: including your primary search term near the beginning of your product's title.

Because Amazon knows their customers use search more than any other method to find products, they place a very high value on what's included in product titles. So, for example, if you're selling a wireless barcode scanner, include that phrase in your title as your primary search term—and preferably in the first five words.

You'd be surprised at how many big brands out there don't know this and instead focus on such things as their brand and model number. But since you *do* know, you'll have a much better chance of out-ranking (and maybe even outselling) those big brands by simply including your search term in the title.

Include other keywords or search terms and benefits in your title, but above all make sure the title makes sense and is easy to read.

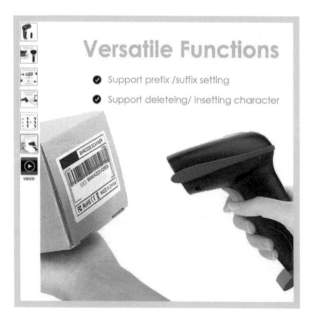

Part 2. Photos

What is the first thing buyers often look at when searching for the right product? Photos.

It's critical to get a few high quality photos of your product. Ideally, use all of the available spots Amazon gives you. For most products, you can upload nine product photos. Nowadays, even the most basic smartphones have incredible cameras, so there's no reason not to have great photos for your product. Just make sure your photos are at least 1,000 pixels by 1,000 pixels, which makes them zoomable on Amazon. (If you want to make things easy, you can simply hire a photographer to take pictures for you.)

For some products such as nutritional supplements, digitally-rendered pictures are more common. For these types of products, you can get high-quality pictures digitally designed by experts you can find on sites such as 99designs.com and Upwork.com.

Part 3. Product description & bullet points

This is your chance to tell potential customers about your product and why they should purchase yours over everyone else's. If you aren't sure about what to put here, let me show you a trick: The best way to figure out what your customers *want* in your product is to see what they *don't like* about your competitor's products. You can do this by reading your competitors' reviews. For example, check out this wireless barcode scanner review.

Salty

★☆☆☆☆ **Model Shown is NOT Bluetooth Capable**
April 26, 2019
Verified Purchase

This item clearly comes up on the Amazon site when Bluetooth is selected on the feature left panel. So this review is for Amazon, I guess or Nadamoo if you have tagged your item this way so it gets viewed. I purchased this and have been using for a while with my laptop, but now as I go to use this with my iPad POS system (which was its ultimate intention) it is not capable and my return window has closed over a week ago. Please remove this from the Bluetooth list so others don't make the same mistake.

In regards to this scanner for USB wireless connectivity, it works very well and I would have given it a 5-star rating.

The above product received a terrible, one star review simply because they didn't make it clear their product is not Bluetooth compatible.

Now that you know this, if you were competing with this product, you could include an instruction manual with your product, and tell future customers that your product "Includes a full color instruction manual to make sure you know exactly how to configure and use your new scanner to Bluetooth."

Another customer had an issue with the scanner not working properly and had trouble getting support to resolve the errors. This gives you an opportunity to talk about your "5-year manufacturer warranty along with world class customer support."

By using the competition's own customer complaints and reviews, you'll know exactly what your customers want and you can tell them exactly why your product is better than anyone else's.

Part 5. Back-end search terms

The last step in creating a highly optimized product listing is a field most sellers don't even know about.

You already know that including your primary search terms in your title is important. Your bullet points are another place to include valuable search terms. But one thing you don't want to do is to start cramming all types of keywords in those two places, because it's going to make your product look "spammy" and turn off buyers.

What do you do if you have more keywords you want your product to show up for, but you don't want to put them in your title or bullet points? You put them in a little known secret field called "Search terms." This field is only visible once you're a seller; you'll find it inside your Amazon Seller Central account. This field allows you to include up to 250 characters of valuable search terms that no one other than you will even know about. You simply include them in this field, separate them with a space, and within a few minutes your product will be ready to show up for keywords that aren't even visible to anyone looking at your listing.

ASIN: B07VZWQGDJ
Product Name: Keto BHB Oil Capsules - BHB exogenous Ketones - Keto Pills to Aid Diet - High Energy Increased Focus- Help Stave Off Hunger Pains and Reach Body Goals- Ketogenic Diet Supplement Pills - 60 Capsules
Manufacturer: Fury Fitness
Brand Name: Fury Fitness
Manufacturer Part Number: KBHB-60Capsules
Package Quantity: 1
Product ID: 850007401054
Product ID Type: upc

Marketplace: US

List Price: $25.87

Competing Marketplace Offers
2 New from $14.95 + $0.00 shipping

Amazon Sales Rank: 49,270

| Vital Info | Variations | Offer | Compliance | Images | Description | Keywords | More Details | Advanced View |

Search Terms ❶ eto BHB Pills Exogenous Ketones Advanced Keto Diet Pills Keto Pills for Energy

Intended Use ❶ Ex: asthma

Add More   Remove Last

To help you remember exactly how to optimize your first product listing, I've put together a **Product Listing Optimization Checklist** which will help guide you through this process. Use this template to create the perfect product listing. As a result, you can attract loads of visitors from Amazon and convert them into buyers that make you sales.

PRODUCT LISTING OPTIMIZATION CHECKLIST

To build a highly optimized product listing, you need to focus on just four parts of your listing.

The Four Parts of an Optimized Listing:

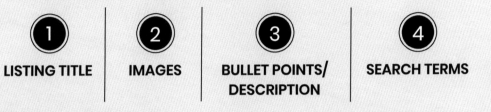

1	**2**	**3**	**4**
LISTING TITLE	IMAGES	BULLET POINTS/ DESCRIPTION	SEARCH TERMS

LISTING TITLE

Include the **main keyword** for your product at the **beginning of your title.** These are the most likely words a customer would use to find your product.

In this example, you can see they have added the main keyword straight after their brand name.

An alternative to this would be to add "Wireless Barcode Scanner by Nadamoo" at the **beginning.**

You should also include other keywords or search terms and benefits in your title, but always make sure the title:

- Is easy to read
- Makes sense

In this example, they have included other search terms and features, but no actual benefits. They should have used some of the benefits from their bullet points.

The next critical features of your listing are your images or photos. Remember, **this is often the first thing buyers look** at when deciding which product to purchase.

Make sure your photos are at least 1000 pixels by 1000 pixels, which makes them zoomable:

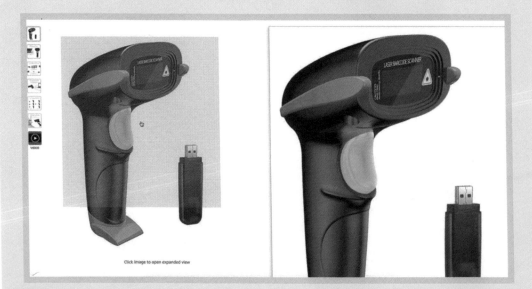

The next critical areas to focus on are your bullet points and product description. This is your chance to tell your potential customers about your product and why they should purchase yours over everyone else's on Amazon.

Make sure your bullet points include: Search terms, benefits, and features of your product.

Then, feel free to include a short bio of your brand in the description.

The best way to figure out what your customers want in your product is to **go look at your competitors and see what people don't like about their products.**

Take a look at this product's reviews:

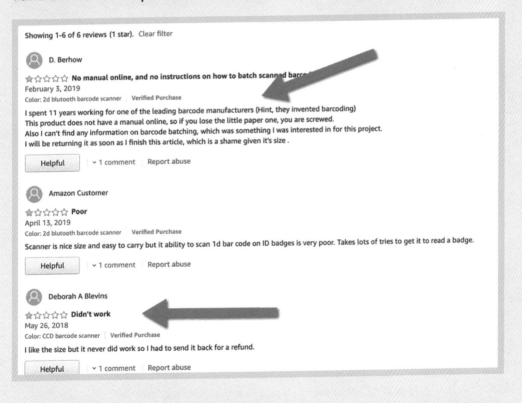

Showing 1-6 of 6 reviews (1 star). Clear filter

D. Berhow

★☆☆☆☆ **No manual online, and no instructions on how to batch scanned barc...**
February 3, 2019
Color: 2d blutooth barcode scanner | Verified Purchase

I spent 11 years working for one of the leading barcode manufacturers (Hint, they invented barcoding)
This product does not have a manual online, so if you lose the little paper one, you are screwed.
Also I can't find any information on barcode batching, which was something I was interested in for this project.
I will be returning it as soon as I finish this article, which is a shame given it's size .

Helpful   ˅ 1 comment   Report abuse

Amazon Customer

★☆☆☆☆ **Poor**
April 13, 2019
Color: 2d blutooth barcode scanner | Verified Purchase

Scanner is nice size and easy to carry but it ability to scan 1d bar code on ID badges is very poor. Takes lots of tries to get it to read a badge.

Helpful   ˅ 1 comment   Report abuse

Deborah A Blevins

★☆☆☆☆ **Didn't work**
May 26, 2018
Color: CCD barcode scanner | Verified Purchase

I like the size but it never did work so I had to send it back for a refund.

Helpful   ˅ 1 comment   Report abuse

This product got a terrible, one-star review simply because they didn't have an instruction manual or any online instructions.

Now that you know this, not only should you make sure to include that with your product, but you could also make sure you tell all your future customers your product "Includes a full color instruction manual to make sure you know exactly how to configure and use your new scanner."

Since another customer had an issue with the scanner working and getting support, you could also talk about your "5-year manufacturer's warranty, along with world-class customer support."

You could include these two issues that your product overcomes in the first two or three bullet points, or even description:

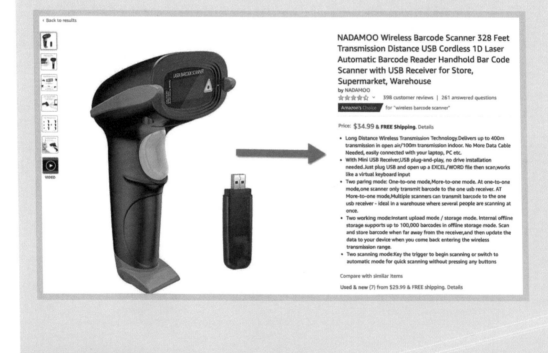

‹ Back to results

NADAMOO Wireless Barcode Scanner 328 Feet Transmission Distance USB Cordless 1D Laser Automatic Barcode Reader Handhold Bar Code Scanner with USB Receiver for Store, Supermarket, Warehouse
by NADAMOO
★★★★☆ ˅   398 customer reviews | 261 answered questions
Amazon's Choice   for "wireless barcode scanner"

Price: $34.99 & FREE Shipping. Details

- Long Distance Wireless Transmission Technology.Delivers up to 400m transmission in open air/100m transmission indoor. No More Data Cable Needed, easily connected with your laptop, PC etc.
- With Mini USB Receiver,USB plug-and-play, no drive installation needed.Just plug USB and open up a EXCEL./WORD file then scan,works like a virtual keyboard input
- Two paring mode: One-to-one mode,More-to-one mode. At one-to-one mode,one scanner only transmit barcode to the one usb receiver. AT More-to-one mode,Multiple scanners can transmit barcode to the one usb receiver - ideal in a warehouse where several people are scanning at once.
- Two working mode:Instant upload mode / storage mode. Internal offline storage supports up to 100,000 barcodes in offline storage mode. Scan and store barcode when far away from the receiver,and then update the data to your device when you come back entering the wireless transmission range.
- Two scanning mode:Key the trigger to begin scanning or switch to automatic mode for quick scanning without pressing any buttons

Compare with similar items

Used & new (7) from $29.99 & FREE shipping. Details

SEARCH TERMS

The last step in creating a highly optimized product listing is a "secret" field that most sellers don't even know about.

We already know that including your search terms in your title, bullet points, and description is important for getting your product to show up when customers are searching on Amazon.

Include additional keywords in the "Search terms" field that is only visible inside your Amazon Seller Central account.

This field allows you to include up to 250 characters of valuable search terms that no one other than you will even know about. You simply include them in this field, separate them with a space, and within a few minutes, your product will be ready to show up for keywords that aren't even visible to anyone looking at your listing.

Follow all these steps, and you will have a competitive advantage over your competitors with very little effort!

How to push your product up in the rankings so buyers see it (and buy it).

Once your product listing page is optimized to convert as many visitors into buyers as possible, it's time to execute four specific marketing strategies that will push your product up in the rankings for high-value keywords.

These strategies include:

- Use Facebook Messenger to start pre-selling your product before it's ready
- Use Facebook to target your ideal customer
- Use Amazon's secret "Prime Day" discount codes to create an offer your customers can't refuse
- Use Amazon Sponsored Product Ads

Strategy #1: Use Facebook Messenger to start pre-selling your product before it's ready

This strategy is one that barely even existed a year ago. It's affordable, simple to set up, and allows you to leverage the incredible power of social media.

When launching your first product, or even your second, fifth, or 10th, it's always much easier if you have a list of potential customers already looking for a product like yours. This used to be incredibly difficult or maybe even impossible for new sellers, but now it's easy, thanks to a free tool called ManyChat.

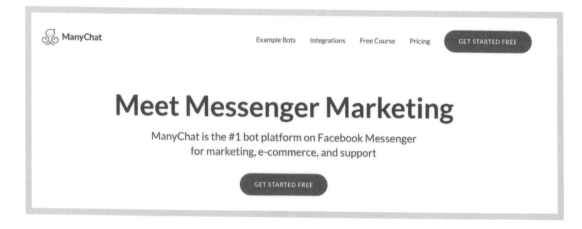

ManyChat is the leading automation tool for Facebook Messenger marketing. It ties into your Facebook page for your brand and can help you build a list of interested potential buyers and communicate with them all at once.

Using this tool, you can start promoting your product weeks before it's ready and have a list of hungry buyers the moment your product arrives on Amazon.

Using a Facebook page for your brand, you can target potential customers who might be interested in your new product. Start by creating a post to get people excited about your new product.

The image below is an example of a post our team created for a new product targeting people who are into Keto. As you can see in the example, you don't even have to have a picture of your product... you just need to post something that will get the attention of your target audience. (In this case it's some healthy looking people who are into fitness.)

In your post, tell everyone that you're launching a brand-new product soon, and if they want to get it as soon as it's released and receive an awesome, exclusive discount on it, simply comment on the post.

Don't worry about having to answer everyone who comments on this post, because that's where ManyChat comes in. Once you have that post created, your next step is to set up an automated responder in ManyChat for anyone who comments on your post.

Using the completely free version of ManyChat, it's pretty simple to do. All you have to do is set up a "Facebook Comments Growth Tool," which automatically responds to people commenting on your posts, and then places them on a list of subscribers that you can notify the moment your new product goes live.

To set this up, you need to follow three simple steps:

Step 1. Tell ManyChat which post you want to respond to comments on. In the example below, I chose the post we'd just created.

This strategy is affordable, simple to set up, and allows you to leverage the incredible power of social media.

Step 2. Create a response confirming that anyone who is commenting on your post really wants to get notified about your product launch. This is an important step and is a requirement by Facebook to make sure you're only sending messages to people who want to receive them.

ManyChat

Fury Fitness   PRO

Dashboard

Audience

Live Chat

Growth Tools

Widgets

Ads   BETA

Broadcasting

Automation

Flows

Settings   ●

Widgets › **Keto Launch**

Facebook Comments

Settings   Auto-response   Opt-In Actions

Message to commenters

Hey [Full Name] ! Just reply "Yes" to confirm you want to be notified the moment our new Keto product goes live and get a crazy discount on it! 🥕

☺ {} 862

This text will be sent to everyone who commented on your post, meeting specified criteria.

ⓘ **Please, Note**
People who comment on your post will become your subscribers on Messenger only after they reply to this message. When they do it, you can send them an Opt-In Message

ⓘ *Be Careful!*

Step 3. Let respondents know that they are signed up and will be notified about your product launch.

Widgets > **Keto Launch**

Save

BETA
Facebook Comments

Settings   Auto-response   Opt-In Actions

Sending options

○ Don't send the opt-in message

○ Send to everyone who replies

● Send only to users who reply with a keyword

| Enter keywords here, separated by commas |

Opt-In Message

| Growth Tool #110 Opt-In M...   ✎ Edit   ⬇ Replace |

Add Subscriber to Sequence

| Enter sequence |

ⓘ *Be Careful! This is an experimental feature.*

Due to technical limitations of Facebook platform, ManyChat can't in some cases identify a user as a

< Back   Fury Fitness >
         Typically replies instantly   Manage

Welcome Mike! 🔵 Thank you for subscribing. The next post is coming soon, stay tuned!

P.S. If you ever want to unsubscribe just type "stop".

Anytime someone comments on the post and wants to get notified about your product launch they'll be added to your list. This is cutting edge technology, and you'll be one of the first to use it in your new business.

To begin, go to https://manychat.com and follow the instructions to get started for free.

Strategy #2: Use Facebook to target your ideal customer

To make sure that the right people see your post about your new product, you can boost your post right from your Facebook page. This can cost as little as $2 a day and allows you to target people using Facebook's simple, yet incredibly powerful targeting tools.

Below the post you created in the previous strategy, you'll see a "Boost" button. When you select that, you can target your ideal customer by telling Facebook what type of people you want to reach. In this example, I'm targeting people who are into Ketones AND like to shop on Amazon.

In the above example, I chose to spend a total of $20, which comes down to $2 a day.

Once you've selected your audience and your budget, you can start the boost... and start building a list of customers on autopilot.

HOW PAUL MILLER CREATED AN IN-DEMAND BRAND PEOPLE CAN'T STOP TALKING ABOUT.

Paul Miller was a 53-year-old ex-Marine, married with three kids in Ashburn, VA, trying to make a living running pizza franchises.

"It was a losing situation," he recalls. "For almost five years, I pleaded with landlords, negotiated with lenders, and worked my butt off traveling from store to store trying to cover manager shifts to save money."

Paul put in hours of grunt work for little pay-off. "Most of the days I was working from 9 a.m. to 10 p.m. The days were long and hard, and at 53, being on my feet all day was not as easy as it used to be. Even though we were headed in the right direction, cash was still extremely tight, and bills were running late."

Paul knew that a single wrong move or stroke of bad luck could wipe him out. And then, in a freak occurrence while playing ball with his kids at Cub Scouts, he broke his collarbone.

"I can clearly remember thinking 'What am I going to do? I may not be able to work... my daughter is going to college soon and I don't know if I'll be able to pay for it. This may be it—total failure.'"

With Amazing as his guide, an Amazon selling business became his Plan B. "During my recovery I dug into all things Amazon. In addition to the ASM course, I participated in a coaching group, listened to every podcast about selling on Amazon, read every blog I could find, joined every Facebook group I could find. There were so many inspiring ASM success stories."

But the question was: what would he sell?

"One night, as I lay in bed, not able to sleep, my mind racing about the future, I turned to my podcasts for inspiration, or at least something to calm my racing mind so I could get back to sleep. But I only had earbuds, and they get very uncomfortable after a while, especially if you're a side sleeper. So I got up that night and began searching for a supplier of sleep headphones."

Paul ordered a small quantity of the sleep headphones he found from suppliers and listed them on Amazon using what he'd learned from ASM. Within a few weeks, the initial order sold out.

"I contacted the manufacturer again to talk about a re-order and how we could improve the speakers and designs. It wasn't long before we were selling 20 per day in different styles and colors."

Shortly after, "I hired a local photographer who could provide some models using our headphones in a variety of situations. One of the shots she took was of her nine-year old daughter using our headphones with her tablet. That was my 'a-ha' moment. I thought, `How cool would it be to make kids headphones in fun character designs?'"

Paul's daughter Helen, an aspiring art student, drew up some designs: a frog, a kitten, a puppy, and a panda. "We decided to start with the frog. I sent the designs to my manufacturer, we went back and forth with samples and prototypes, and by November we had them selling on Amazon. We sold out for the holidays."

Paul called his new brand CozyPhones, and the response was incredible. "As the product reviews started coming in we knew we had something special." Kids loved them. Parents loved them. And it turned out the product suited an unexpected niche: kids with special needs.

"My next door neighbor is an elementary school special education teacher. One day, she explained to me that many of her kids could not tolerate regular earbuds or headphones. I gave her some samples to try. Meanwhile, I joined Facebook groups for Autism and Sensory Processing disorders and began offering samples for review. The results were amazing. Emails and reviews came pouring in. One mother wrote a long email expressing her appreciation for CozyPhones, explaining that before, her son could not participate in some school activities because he could not wear regular headphones."

The momentum continued, and licensing deals with Disney and Nickelodeon (including the popular kids show Paw Patrol) soon followed.

In his first year, Paul's business did $200,000. The following year, $1.9 million. The next year, $4 million.

CozyPhones are now sold on Amazon's U.S. and European marketplaces, Walmart.com, Ebay.com, CozyPhones.com, and more. And Paul's just getting started. "We aspire to scale this business to every Amazon marketplace worldwide and to do over $10 million in sales next year. Long term, I would like to see CozyPhones as a household brand and have them available everywhere our customers want to buy."

Strategy #3: Use Amazon's secret "Prime Day" to create an offer your customer's can't refuse.

Once your list is built and your product is ready to sell, the next step is to create an offer that your customers can't pass up.

To do that, you can take advantage of a marketing tool that Amazon introduced on Prime Day 2019 (the biggest Prime Day in their history). During that Prime Day, Amazon wanted to reward it's 100 Million plus Prime Members by creating discounts specifically for them. To do this they created "Prime Exclusive Discounts" and let sellers like us use them for the first time ever.

What most sellers don't know—and you're one of the first to find out—is that those discounts can *still* be created and used today.

In the image below, you can see what a Prime Exclusive Discount looks like right now. You'll be hard pressed to find these on Amazon because so few people even know you can still use them.

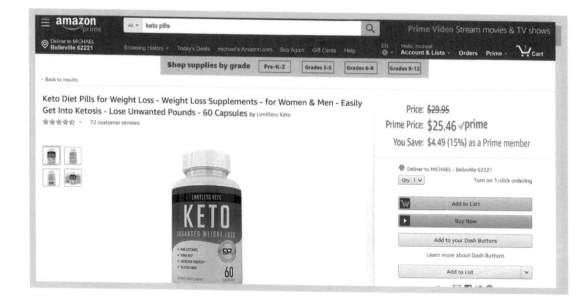

Here's how to create one yourself.

From inside of your Seller Central Account, select "Prime Discounts" under your advertising menu. Then select "Create Discount," and give your discount any name you want. Don't worry, this won't be seen anywhere but by you. (As you can see in the example to the right I've called mine "Keto Launch Discount.")

amazon seller central   ▷   Fury Fitness 🖼   www.amazon.com ▼ | English ▼ | Search   🔍 Messages | Help | Settings

Catalog   Inventory   Pricing   Orders   Advertising   Stores   Programs   Reports   Performance

⚠ **Creating multiple promotions and discounts on the same product may result in customers combining them for significant discounts. Please click Learn More for more information.**

Prime Deals and Discounts   >   Create a Prime Exclusive Discount

Step 1 of 3: Enter discount details

What did you want to name this discount?

| Keto Launch Discount |

Discount start date   Discount end date

📅 MM/DD/YYYY   📅 MM/DD/YYYY

| Save Discount Details | Save and Add Products |

Next, you need to tell Amazon when this discount should start and end, and which products you want to discount. To do this, Amazon gives you a simple spreadsheet to use. Simply upload the spreadsheet, review that everything looks good, and then submit the discount so it will automatically go live on the date you want it to.

Prime Deals and Discounts   >   Keto Launch Discount   >   Add Products   >   Review discount

Step 3 of 3: Review your discounts

Keto Launch Discount   Edit Discount Details

Page | 1 | of 1 | Go | | 10 results per page   ∨

Product details

SKU	Discount Type	↑↓	Prime Discount		Minimum Price		Status	↑	
C8-W7V1-P13N	Percent Off ∨		30.00	%	$ 10.00		Ready to Submit		Remove Product

Page | 1 | of 1 | Go | | 10 results per page   ∨

Add More Products | Save Discount | | Submit Discounts |

And there you have it. By doing this, you're taking advantage of features that practically no one on Amazon even knows about right now!

Strategy #4: Use Amazon Sponsored Products Ads.

At this point, you're almost ready to launch your product. But first, you'll want to do one more thing to ensure your product gets in front of people who are ready to buy.

Your listing should already be optimized for your primary search terms, and that in of itself will help you rank once the sales start coming in. But you can jumpstart that process and make sure your product gets to the top of the searches immediately by using something called Amazon Sponsored Products Ads. These ads let you tell Amazon what search terms your product should show up for and are the easiest way to start getting immediate search rank increases.

To set your first one up you simply head into your Amazon Seller account and go to Advertising > Campaigns > Create new campaign > Sponsored Products.

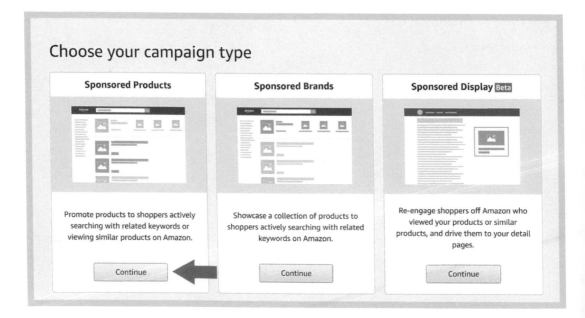

To set up your ads, you first need to give your campaign a name. In the example shown here, I called my campaign "Keto Launch."

Create campaign

Settings

Campaign name ⓘ

Keto Launch

Portfolio ⓘ

No Portfolio

Create portfolios to organize campaig
budget caps, and track performance.

Start ⓘ

Oct 25, 2019

End ⓘ

No end date

Choosing no end date means your car
run longer, and a longer timeframe ca
better insights on search terms and ke
performance to further optimize your

Daily budget ⓘ

$

Most campaigns with a budget over $
throughout the day.

Targeting

Next, select a daily budget for how much you want to spend on ads. There's no reason to go crazy; you can start off with just $10 - $20 in the beginning to try it out.

Once that's done, select "Manual Targeting," and give your Ad Group a name. (Don't worry too much about this; it doesn't matter what you call it.) After that, tell Amazon which product you want to advertise. In this example, I've selected the new Keto product.

Settings

Ad group name ⓘ

Keto Pills

Products ⓘ

Search   Enter list   Upload New

BHB

Sort by date added   Descending ˅

Add all on this page

Keto BHB Oil Capsules - BHB exogenous
Ketones - Keto Pills to Aid Diet - High Energy
⭐⭐⭐⭐⭐(20) $29.99 $16.95 In stock
ASIN: B07VZWQGDJ SKU: FURY-KETO-60-1X

Added

1 product

Keto BHB Oil Capsules - BHB exogenous Ketones -
Keto Pills to Aid Diet - High Energy Increased Focus-
⭐⭐⭐⭐⭐(20) $29.99 $16.95 In stock
ASIN: B07VZWQGDJ SKU: FURY-KETO-60-1X

✕

Back to campaign selection

Cancel   Save as draft   Launch campaign

Now this is the most important part: you need to tell Amazon *which* keyword you want to rank for. In this example, I've chosen "keto diet pill" with "exact match," because I want the product to show up when customers are searching for this exact search term on Amazon.

1 keyword added						
Keyword	Match type ⓘ	Suggested bid ⓘ	Apply all	Keyword bid ⓘ		Remove all
keto diet pills	Exact	$0.68 ⓘ $0.51-$1.36	Apply	$ 0.75		Remove

When you're done, submit your campaign.

Once those ads are turned on, your product will start showing up for your primary search term within a few hours.

Time for launch!

When you've executed the above four strategies and you're ready to launch, send a broadcast message to your ManyChat list from inside the tool's dashboard. Your broadcast will let everyone know your product is now for sale and you've put together an incredible launch price just for them.

By sending out this notification using Facebook Messenger, you'll reach more people than you ever could with emails or ads, since we've all been conditioned to have our phones with us at all times and we're constantly checking for messages.

This quick burst of sales will help you start moving up in the search ranks within a few days, and you can continue using your Sponsored Products Ads for the next week or two in order to continue moving up for your primary search term.

As a result of the product launch steps you've taken, you'll see your product moving up higher and higher in the searches. Soon your product will start selling all on it's own. Why? Because you know how to launch a product using cutting edge strategies that most sellers don't even know exist.

In the next chapter, you'll learn how to put all of this together to build a scalable, profitable, valuable business to achieve any financial goal you want.

FAQ: IS THE MARKET OVERSATURATED?

Every single year, Amazon is growing by an *increasing* amount of sales. For example, for the five years from 2008 to 2013, Amazon grew from $19 billion a year to $74 billion a year in revenue. That's an average annual growth of $11 billion per year. For the next five years, Amazon grew from $74 billion a year to $233 billion a year in revenue. That's an average annual growth of $32 billion per year, or three times more than the previous five years!

There are more opportunities today on Amazon than ever before. You don't have to rank in the top spot or even top 10 spots for a keyword to profit on Amazon. Rankings all the way down the first page make sales.

Considering that less than 20% of all retail happens online today, this opportunity is just getting started. Some people like to say that the market is oversaturated, but this couldn't be further from the truth. Now is a great time to start a business, build a real brand, and sell products online.

With any opportunity, you want to get in when it's growing, not when it's plateaued or, even worse, going down. If you start today, you're in the right phase of the growth cycle to produce great results. Starting now ensures you can ride the trend from brick-and-mortar retail to ecommerce while building your business.

If you wait, you won't may not this advantage.

YOUR NEXT ACTION: PLAN YOUR PRODUCT LISTING.

Using what you learned in this chapter, plan everything you'll need for a killer product listing:

- Title
- Pictures
- Bullet points & description
- Back-end search terms

Remember, it's better to get started than wait, even if you don't have things 100% perfect. Decide on a title, take your pictures, write out your bullet points, description and search terms. Now you're prepared to list your product.

If you don't have a product ready or in-production yet, then *plan* out what you would include for your main product listing elements. This exercise shows you how much you've learned and what you may need to review to be ready to launch your first product.

CREATE YOUR DREAM LIFE: YOUR BLUEPRINT TO SCALE YOUR BUSINESS TO ACHIEVE ANY GOAL.

05

● **In the first four chapters of this book, you've learned a lot.**

Together, we've covered...

1. The amazing opportunity that is waiting for you *right now* to create your own business, build your own brand, and finally live the kind of life you want to live, making the kind of money you want to make.

2. How to find a great product opportunity and choose the right product to sell.

3. How to find a high-quality supplier, either in the US or internationally.

4. How to successfully sell your products online to loads of eager buyers, even with your new brand that no one has ever heard of before.

Now, in this chapter, I'll show you the blueprint to put all of this together so you can build a business that meets your financial and lifestyle dreams.

REMEMBER:

The goal is to build a successful brand, not an "Amazon business". Amazon is a great place to start and produce sales, but your ultimate goal should be to build multiple profitable sales channels.

How much do you want to invest?

Some businesses require a lot of money to start and the risk is unbearable for most. A typical fee for a franchise is $20,000 to $50,000. Then, there's up to $5,000 for legal and accounting fees plus more for working capital, build-out costs for the space, and supplies. You might even need an additional $20,000 to $150,000 for inventory just to get your franchise off the ground!

Starting a restaurant isn't any better. The median cost to open a restaurant is $275,000, and most restaurants fail within the first two years.

Some other businesses are just as expensive. For example, a friend of my family wanted to start her own day spa and was held up trying to get a loan from the Small Business Administration to buy an expensive cosmetic laser machine which cost $150,000!

I want to help as many people achieve financial freedom without going into debt or taking on a crazy amount of risk to do so. I want you to be wealthy, happy, and living life the way you want, not so stressed you can't sleep at night because of the financial risk.

For this business, you really only have a few necessary expenses to get started. The primary expense is inventory. Your inventory is the main asset you're buying to sell at a profit. Your inventory expense includes the cost of the product, packaging, and shipping the product to Amazon's warehouses.

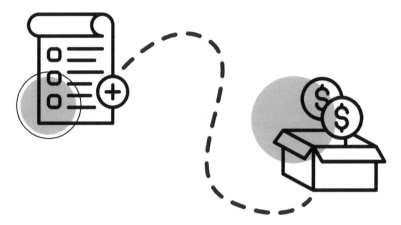

You don't have to start with a lot of money. In fact, I recommend you *don't* risk a bunch of money at first, even if you have some to spare. Start small and slowly build up—it's the smartest way to build your business.

If money is tight, you can start this business with as little as $500 in inventory, including product costs, packaging, and shipping to Amazon. You'll need to search harder for less expensive products and negotiate with suppliers to get them to let you start with only 100 units or so, but it's absolutely possible.

If you have a bit more money to start, spending up to $2,500 or more in initial inventory gives you more options—more products to choose from and more suppliers to work with.

HOW DAVID AND LEAH CUPPS BECAME 30-SOMETHING MILLIONAIRES BY SELLING THEIR BRAND.

Leah and David are a married couple living in Indianapolis, IN. Today, they're millionaires. But it wasn't long ago that they were working as hard as possible to produce a combined income of $100,000 per year, wishing for something *more*.

Prior to starting their online business with the model you're learning about in this book, Leah was a freelance graphic designer, and David a medical sales representative. The couple had also tried running a photo booth rental company together. "The business was successful, but never produced more than $40,000 a year in revenue. We attended 90% of the photo booth events ourselves, because we never had success with dependable employees."

They dreamed of something bigger, something other people might have thought impossible: becoming millionaires by the time they were 40.

To achieve their vision, they knew they'd have to try something different.

Together, they explored the concept of selling products online. "We started before we took ASM, just by using the free content we found on YouTube. Our first product was a seaweed powder. We ordered all the pieces in bulk: seaweed powder, labels, jars, heat wraps. We assembled the first 500 units in our temporary apartment by hand."

They saw the potential in the business, but knew there must be a better way to make it work. "Once we started taking the ASM course, so many more possibilities opened up for us." Using what they learned, they found a product with a high BSR and low competition. "Our first product came from Canada and shipped via FedEx, so it was easy. We just Googled it. Then we posted the product, gave it to friends and family for reviews and started running Amazon ads."

In just two short years, Leah and David were happy to report their business was "doing $2.8 million in revenue."

That's when they started to think that maybe they could sell the brand they'd built so quickly.

"We heard that some people were selling their businesses to investors, so at the end of 2016, we put our business up for sale through a broker. Within a few weeks, we had a full price offer and ended up selling the business for $4 million."

That was a huge turning point for the couple. "To go from earning just over $100,000 a year in 2014, to becoming millionaires three short years later was an incredible experience. Not to mention, we had the freedom and flexibility to work when we wanted and spend time with our family all along the way."

Since then, they've created new brands with about 30 new products. "We launched three new brands in 2017, right after we sold. We plan to sell the businesses in the fall of 2020 for nearly double what we sold the first company for."

David and Leah say it all comes down to having a vision. "Create a compelling vision for where you see the business and your life in one year, three years, and five years from now. A vision that is strong enough that it can pull you through all the obstacles that come along. Part of our vision was to be millionaires by age 40, and we accomplished that by age 38. If we didn't have that goal in mind, we would have never built the business to the size it became."

Remember Justin and Channing who you read about in Chapter 1? They started their business with $2,000 in inventory for their first product and just $500 for their second product. Today, they produce over $500,000 per month in sales selling 68 products in three different marketplaces.

Here's another example from Mike McClary—who's now our Chief Product Officer. A few years ago, Mike had a successful job as a Finance Director for a telecommunications company. Mike liked his job and the people he worked with. But something was missing. Too often he found himself staying in hotel rooms while visiting clients on the road instead of being with his family back home.

He didn't want to miss any more of his daughter and son's lives. He wanted to be there to take them to school, pick them up, and see their tennis games. He wanted to control his schedule and be able to work from home. Plus, he didn't see how he could ever retire and have the freedom he wanted for himself and his family unless he built something of his own.

Mike got started with the business model you're learning about in this book through our ASM program. But he didn't want to risk a bunch of money on his first business. So he started with only $500 in inventory. Within a year, he was producing enough income from his business to quit his finance job. Since then, he's gone on to sell multiple millions per year with his brands, even selling as much as $250,000 in a single day.

Mike was so grateful for the transformation in his life because of the business he built, he decided to start working with us at Amazing to help thousands more people achieve freedom. Today, Mike is our Chief Product Officer and works with us every day to change lives around the world while still running his successful ecommerce business.

It's up to you to decide how much you're willing to invest in your business to get started. You can start with as little as $500 in inventory like Mike. Or, as we recommend, you can start with a bit more so you have more products to choose from and more money to advertise your product for faster initial growth. If possible, we recommend an initial budget of $1,500 to $3,000 for inventory and marketing. However, the most important thing is to get started as soon as possible. Start with whatever amount you're comfortable with that gets you started *now*.

FAQ: HOW MANY PRODUCTS SHOULD I SELL TO MAXIMIZE MY PROFITS?

No matter what your goals are, I always recommend staying focused with your business. This means one single brand and, at first, one single product. This allows you to produce the best results possible in the least amount of time possible.

Sometimes, a single product under a single brand can meet your financial goals.

(One example of this is Anne Ferris from Costa Rica. She has a single product that sells $100,000 a month. That product alone is enough to provide a significant income for her and her family.)

There are thousands of products on Amazon that sell $100,000 a month or more—some even sell into the millions per month! So don't spread yourself too thin in the beginning, and don't assume that one product isn't enough to make you some good money.

How much profit can I make? (And how can I increase my profits?)

Let's talk profit.

You can't fund your freedom with sales. Profit is the key.

Without profit, you're doing a bunch of work without any change in your freedom or income.

A typical bottom-line profit margin in this business after all product costs, shipping costs, advertising, and Amazon fees is 20-40%. That means for every $10,000 you sell, you can potentially make $2,000 to $4,000 in income.

You might decide to reinvest in your business to grow it faster or hire staff to give you more freedom, which might affect your profit from time-to-time. But a 20-40% estimate to start with is a good general guideline when you're just getting started.

Once you have a product established, managing the business takes very little time. Because Amazon takes care of most of the customer service and all of the shipping and processing, your only jobs are to: make sure your inventory stays in stock, keep marketing your products to stay ahead of competitors, and respond to the few customer service emails that come through Amazon.

Once established, it's possible to manage your entire business using this model in an hour or two a day. Later, you can hire a staff member to take over some of the tasks so your time required is even less and you can truly live the *4-hour workweek* lifestyle.

> # With enough time, effort, and the right strategies, you can grow your business as big as you want.

With enough time, effort, and the right strategies, you can grow your business as big as you want. To scale your sales bigger and bigger, you only need to do more marketing, add more products to your brand, or sell in more places. (Of the three, the most efficient and easiest way to increase sales is to do more marketing for your existing product because it takes the least amount of time and effort.) While any one of these can increase your sales significantly, if you combine all three—and put in the time and effort— you can achieve any financial goal you want.

While I'd encourage you start with just one product (see FAQ: How many products should I sell to maximize my profits?), most people eventually choose to expand their brands. I recommend staying with products in the same market that can be sold under the same brand. That way, each new product you sell can be sold to all the people who have already bought from you. This makes growing sales even easier and faster.

When you're ready, you can increase sales by selling on Amazon marketplaces in other countries. Or you can sell the same products outside of Amazon on your own online store. Or both. No matter what you do, remember: the goal is to build a successful brand, not an

"Amazon business." Amazon is a great place to start and produce sales, but your ultimate goal should be to build multiple profitable sales channels.

You can keep expanding for as long and as big as you want until you achieve your goals.

YOUR NEXT ACTION: SET SPECIFIC GOALS.

Get clear on what your end-goal is:

- How much money do you want to make every month?
- Do you ultimately want to sell the business/brand you create? If so, what is your goal selling price?

Don't let yourself be wishy-washy on this. Take some time to reflect. Run some numbers if you want to. Figure out what you want, write it down, and start working towards it right now.

Then try out our *Dream Goal Calculator* tool to see how many units you need to sell per month, per week, and per year to achieve your goals at **www.MillionDollarBrandBook.com/dream**

TARGET MONTHLY INCOME GOAL	$10,000
Product selling price	**$34.99** per unit
Product cost	**$13.00** per unit
Net profit using FBA Revenue Calculator	**$14.66** per unit
NUMBER OF UNITS SOLD TO ACHIEVE GOAL	
Per month	**682** units
Per week	**171** units
Per day	**23** units

YOUR 12-MONTH ROADMAP TO **FINANCIAL FREEDOM.**

Wow. You've now learned how to choose products, create your own brand, source high-quality suppliers, beat even the biggest brands for sales, and chart a course for your business goals. Best of all, you haven't only learned what to do—you've *applied it*, by taking action at the end of each chapter.

That said, I recognize that all this information can still feel a bit overwhelming. Starting a business takes consistent, steady effort, so it's important to stay the course. With that in mind, I've created a 12-month roadmap for you to follow.

This roadmap outlines exactly what to do each month to create the greatest success for your business. Follow these steps and at the end of the year, you'll have a business in place that delivers the financial and lifestyle freedom you've been dreaming about.

Your 12-Month Roadmap: What to do each month to achieve business success.

MONTH 1

- Research products.
- Narrow product list down to your top three options.
- Contact suppliers for pricing information.
- Choose top one product option.
- Order 2-3 samples from different suppliers.
- Evaluate samples.
- Choose the best supplier.
- Create a brand name and logo.
- Place first inventory order. (Pay 30% down payment.)
- Setup Amazon Seller Central account.

MONTH 2

- Prepare social media profiles for brand: Facebook, Instagram, YouTube (optional), & Twitter (optional).

- Research best keywords for Amazon product listing.

- Plan title, bullets, and description for product listing.

- Plan content for 9 product photos. (Primary photo should have a plain white background.)

- Begin posting on social media accounts about your upcoming product release.

- (Optional) Run a small ad budget (e.g., $5-$10/day) to attract followers to one of your social media accounts.

- Check on your inventory order (might take a full 4-5 weeks to prepare).

MONTH 3

- Your inventory ships! If arriving by sea, will take an additional 5 weeks. If arriving by air, will only take 7-10 days to arrive at Amazon. If being shipped from inside the US, will only take 2 -3 days to arrive.

- Create a simplified Amazon product listing with a temporary picture and temporary text so you can ship inventory into Amazon.

- (If your product is being manufactured overseas) When your inventory is ready to be shipped, contact a freight forwarder to get your inventory from the supplier to Amazon's Fulfillment by Amazon (FBA) warehouses.

- (If your product is being manufactured in the US) Contact your supplier and arrange shipping of the inventory to Amazon FBA.

- Continue posting on your social media profiles - aim to build an audience of least 100 people.

- Order a UPC code for your new product (get our up-to-date recommended service here: www.MillionDollarBrandBook.com/upc).

MONTH 4

- (When your inventory arrives) Get product photos of your new product.

- Your product should be at Amazon's FBA warehouses this month and ready for sale!

- Create your final listing with great product photos, a great title, well-written bullets, and a compelling product description.

- Setup your automated customer follow-up email system with a tool such as ManageByStats's SellerMail (www.MillionDollarBrandBook.com/mbs).

- Do a promotion to friends and family — or to the audience you've built on social media — to get your first 3-5 product reviews on Amazon.

Start your product launch with a time-limited coupon (e.g., 30% off), Amazon Sponsored Product Ads advertising, Facebook ads (optional), and social media postings. Run this launch for 7-10 days to get initial sales.

TWO ADDITIONAL SUCCESS SECRETS (THAT ARE ALSO ESSENTIAL FOR HAPPINESS.)

Before you go, there are two more critical components to success that are worthy of mention: Relationships and helping others.

After over ten years creating businesses, succeeding, and failing, I've found these are key ingredients in not only becoming successful, but also enjoying and making the most out of the wealth and freedom you're about to create for yourself.

First, let's look at the importance of relationships.

In 1938, scientists started a study to track the health of 268 Harvard students during the Great Depression. They hoped to track these individuals' lives to gain an understanding of leading healthy and happy lives.

Some of these students became successful businessmen, doctors, and lawyers; others became alcoholics and schizophrenics.

What did they find after following these people for nearly their entire lives? Robert Waldinger, director of the Harvard Study of Adult Behavior says, "The clearest message we get from this 75-year study is this: Good relationships keep us happier and healthier. Period."

We spend so much time trying to achieve things: buy this car, buy that house. And there's nothing wrong with that. But let's not forget that *things* don't make us happy. In fact, we'd be far happier and healthier long-term if we focused on building better, deeper relationships. Loneliness, according to Waldinger, is as harmful to your health as smoking and alcoholism.

As you apply the methods you've learned about in this book, one of the biggest benefits you'll experience is having the financial and lifestyle freedom to spend time with those who matter to you: your family, your friends, and others that enrich your life. (You might also use the same freedoms to avoid spending time with toxic people such as possibly someone in your workplace you work at now to pay the bills.)

Choose positive friends and positive family members who you feel good around. Make a list of those people and set reminders to stay in-touch with them. Reach out to a family member or friend you haven't spoken to in years. As Waldinger says, "The good life is built with relationships."

Why help others?

Helping others is more than just a nice thing to do. (And you should do it—we're all in this together.) But there's also a circular effect to altruism.

Doing good for others makes us feel better.

When we feel better, we're more positive and optimistic. When we're more positive and optimistic, we take bigger risks, act more confidently, have more energy, and more firmly pursue our goals. This makes us more successful.

Therefore, doing good for others does good for ourselves.

It's not that you're expecting something in return by helping a friend. You're not expecting them to help you the next day, though they likely will. You're giving to them without expecting anything in return. This makes you feel good. Then, the other benefits that come back to you cascade from there.

Everytime you help someone, you deposit into a bank of goodwill. Eventually, when *you* need something, you can make a withdrawal from that plentiful bank. If you're selfish, on the other hand, you never have any resources to tap into. You live in a lonely, threatening reality, though you're in the same world as everyone else.

Helping others without expecting anything in return almost always does return *something* for you. It either returns a feeling of satisfaction and positivity which creates more success for you. Or, it returns positive actions of others toward you in the future when you're in need.

As your success, financial or otherwise, continues to grow, look around you. Find ways to pay it forward. Helping others is a part of success.

And like anything else, you don't have to wait until you have millions of dollars or more time to make a positive impact. With a simple act of kindness, you can start today.

MONTH 5

- Continue promoting your product with Amazon advertising, social media, and great customer service.
- Monitor and respond to customer reviews (good and bad) on your product listing.
- Monitor your inventory levels and reorder when your inventory gets low.
- Continue building and nurturing your social media followings.
- If you haven't already, setup an email capture system and start collecting emails as well to send out future discounts and new product deals (get our recommended services at www.MillionDollarBrandBook.com/email).
- (Optional) Create a simple brand website using a tool such as Wix or Shopify.

MONTH 6

- By now, you will likely need to reorder inventory if you haven't already. Based on your current sales volume, how long it takes for your inventory to get manufactured, and how long it takes to ship, you should be able to estimate how many units you need to reorder. Do that now and place your next order of inventory if necessary.
- Evaluate feedback from customers to see if you need to or can improve any aspect of your current product when you reorder.
- Start looking for additional product opportunities that fit your brand. Specifically, look for products people are buying that are already buying your first product using Amazon's "Frequently Bought Together" and "Customers Who Bought this Also Bought" information.
- Ask your supplier what other similar products they manufacture that might be good opportunities.
- Find the best possible next product to sell that fits your brand and has good profit potential.
- Order samples of your next product opportunity.
- Apply for a trademark for your brand so you can get Brand Registry (we recommend legalzoom.com or Amazon's new IP Accelerator program to get your trademark).

MONTH 7

- Continue promoting your first product with Amazon advertising, social media, and any other traffic source you want to try.
- Track marketing results. Scale what works and throw out what doesn't.
- Evaluate samples of your second potential product.
- Order inventory for your second product.
- Plan out the listing for your second product including images, title, bullets, and description.
- Let your audience know—especially current customers—that you have a new product coming and you're going to give them a special discount when it comes out.

MONTH 8

- Create a new simplified Amazon product listing for your second product like you did for your first product so you can ship inventory to Amazon when it's ready.
- Keep providing great customer service and monitoring your reviews, traffic, and sales for your first product.
- Continue engaging with your social media followers to keep your accounts active so you can have a successful launch of your second product.

MONTH 9

- Around this time, you might get your second product live.
- Like with your first, you want to get great product photos for this product too.
- Create your final listing for your second product.
- Plan and execute a big promotion for your second product, making sure to give a special discount to customers who bought your first product (they're your best source of quick sales).

MONTH 10

- Monitor your inventory levels of your first two products.
- If cash flow allows, continue to look for 1-2 additional products to add to your brand that you can sell to existing customers and use to bring in new customers.
- As your sales for existing products grow and you place larger orders, negotiate with your suppliers for better pricing and payment terms.

MONTH 11

- Consider adding package inserts inside your product packaging that cross-promote the other products your brand sells.

- Continue providing exceptional customer service to get good reviews, encourage repeat buying, and get referral sales.

- If you're making good, consistent sales on Amazon, you might consider expanding where you sell to either your own website using a platform such as Shopify or adding another marketplace such as Walmart.com.

- You might also consider expanding internationally to sell on multiple Amazon marketplaces across the world including Amazon.com, Amazon.co.uk, Amazon.de, Amazon.jp, and more.

MONTH 12

- Celebrate and reflect on your first full year as a business owner! You've done what most people only dream of - you've built a business you own, taking action, pushing through challenges, and creating the life *you* want.

- Next, start thinking about the future: what do you want to accomplish *next* year? Think about and write down your goals. Here are some to consider for the next 12 months: an annual profit target, a monthly profit amount, a monthly income to receive from your business, a certain number of products for sale, to quit your job, or to enjoy the freedom your business provides you by going on a vacation or buying something for yourself.

- Lastly, start thinking about building a *team*. If you're doing everything yourself, you own a *job*, not a business. When your business is producing consistent profits, start planning your first hire so you can free your time up and own a company that can run without you. Building a team of people to help run and grow a business you own is one of the most important keys to true financial freedom.

YOUR NEXT ACTION: START YOUR 12-MONTH ROADMAP NOW.

The first step in your 12-month roadmap doesn't start in January... or next month... or next year. It starts right now. (In fact, I'm hoping you've *already* started by following the action items in this book.)

It's important that you follow this roadmap. Don't let it fall to the wayside. Add the roadmap actions to your calendar, and/or print out the roadmap and hang it by your desk so you can see it everyday. For a handy printable version of the roadmap, go here: **www.MillionDollarBrandBook.com/roadmap**

CONCLUSION:
DO THIS **NOW.**

Congratulations. By reading this book from start to finish, you've done something many people aren't willing to do: commit to taking action to create the life you want for yourself.

Along the way, you've not only learned, you've put what you learned into *action*. And that's a critical, essential component for success.

Now, let's recap what we've covered together.

In **Chapter 1**, you learned that today is the best time in history to build a business, especially an ecommerce business selling products online. Brick-and-mortar retail still captures over 80% of sales, but sales are moving online fast. By starting a business online now, you're in a great position to profit for years to come.

In **Chapter 2**, you learned that it all starts with choosing a great, high-quality product. You also learned that Amazon, the world's largest online retailer, makes finding great product opportunities incredibly simple—if you know what you're looking for.

In **Chapter 3**, you learned that whatever product you decide to sell, you must own the brand. When you own the brand, you control how it's sold, where it's sold, and how much money you sell it for. Plus, you own a valuable asset that's worth real money to someone looking to buy it in the future. You also learned how easy it is to build your own branded version of just about any product sold online. Then you learned how to find high-quality suppliers using Google and Alibaba.

In **Chapter 4**, you learned how to make sales—even for a brand new product—using Prime Discounts, Facebook Messenger, and Amazon's internal advertising system. Combining these tools in a systematic marketing promotion helps push your product high in the rankings for popular search terms on Amazon.

In **Chapter 5**, you created a blueprint for your own success. You decided how much you're willing to invest, calculated your potential profit margin, learned how to scale your business, and set some clear goals for yourself.

I've given you what you need to get started. But before you go, I have one more bit of advice for you. And it's important.

> # Don't wait. The best time to start on your path to success is 10 years ago. The second best is now.

If you ask someone who is 25 when they wished they would have started focusing more on what matters, they'll tell you at 15 years old.

Someone who is 45 will tell you at 35.

Someone who is 75 will tell you at 65, or earlier.

Not to sound morbid, but we often don't grasp our own mortality until it's too late. We wait until a near death experience or the death of a family member and then, maybe, we realize that time is slipping by every day.

The average lifespan of a person living in the US is less than 79 years. So if you're 35 years old, for example, and you live the average amount of time, you have only 44 years left. That's 44 summers, 44 winters, 44 springs, and 44 falls left. If you see your parents or brother or sister or good friend only once per year, you will only see them 44 more times.

On the other hand, if you start today, work hard, change your actions, and in two years your life is completely different, you can live another 42 years with the amazing life you've always wanted.

Or, you can stay where you're at, keep doing what you're doing, and live another 44 years with regret, wishing you would have done something different "when you were younger."

As Steve Jobs once said, "Remembering you are going to die is the best way I know to avoid the trap of thinking you have something to lose. You are already naked. There is no reason not to follow your heart."

No matter how old you are, you'll never have more time left to change your life than you have today.

So get out there and get started now.

Important: Do This Now

You're well on your way to creating a life of freedom. You've finished this powerful book and now understand what's possible when you follow the right business model that's worked for so many people before you.

What's next?

I want to make sure you succeed. So my team and I have prepared a special video walkthrough of how to build this exact business—and we're giving it to you for FREE.

In this video series, you'll see:

- A live demonstration of researching and finding the best product opportunities on Amazon with our 5 criteria

- Step-by-step instructions on how to find high-quality suppliers for any product you want using sites such as Alibaba.com

- A walkthrough of planning and executing a successful launch of a new product to rank at the top of Amazon and beat the biggest brands in the world

- And much, much more!

Plus, you'll get additional free bonuses with each video in the series you can use to build your own successful brand and finally achieve financial freedom.

Get instant access to this video series here now:
www.MillionDollarBrandBook.com/launch

This is my gift to you for reading this book.

It's been a pleasure to share this journey with you. I can't wait to hear about your success and maybe even meet you one day.

To Your Success,

Matt Clark

Matt Clark
Co-founder & Chairman of Amazing.com, Inc.
Connect with Matt on Instagram or Twitter: @mattclarktx